THE FUTURE OF
THE AMERICAN NEGRO

THE FUTURE OF
THE AMERICAN NEGRO

Booker T. Washington

AFRO-AMERICAN STUDIES

Published by The New American Library

AFRO-AMERICAN STUDIES
are published by
The New American Library, Inc.,
1301 Avenue of the Americas, New York, New York 10019

First Printing, September, 1969

PRINTED IN THE UNITED STATES OF AMERICA

PREFACE.

In giving this volume to the public, I deem it fair to say that I have yielded to the oft-repeated requests that I put in some more definite and permanent form the ideas regarding the Negro and his future which I have expressed many times on the public platform and through the public press and magazines.

I make grateful acknowledgment to the "Atlantic Monthly" and "Appleton's Popular Science Monthly" for their kindness in granting permission for the use of some part of articles which I have at various times contributed to their columns.

BOOKER T. WASHINGTON.

Tuskegee Normal and Industrial Institute,
Tuskegee, Ala., October 1, 1899.

CONTENTS.

Contents

Contents

Contents

The Future of the American Negro

CHAPTER I.

In this volume I shall not attempt to give the origin and history of the Negro race either in Africa or in America. My attempt is to deal only with conditions that now exist and bear a relation to the Negro in America and that are likely to exist in the future. In discussing the Negro, it is always to be borne in mind that, unlike all the other inhabitants of America, he came here without his own consent; in fact, was compelled to leave his own country and become a part of another through physical force. It should also be borne in mind, in our efforts to change and improve the present condition of the Negro, that we are dealing with a race which had little necessity to labour in its native country. After being brought to America, the Negroes were forced to labour for about 250 years under circumstances which were calculated not to inspire them with love and respect for labour. This constitutes a part of the reason why I insist that it is necessary to emphasise the matter of industrial education as a means of giving the black man the foundation of a civilisation upon which he will grow and prosper. When I speak of industrial education, however, I wish it always understood that I mean, as did General Armstrong, the founder of the Hampton Institute, for thorough academic and religious training to go side by side with industrial training. Mere training of the hand without the culture of brain and heart would mean little.

The first slaves were brought into this country by the Dutch in 1619, and were landed at Jamestown, Virginia. The first cargo consisted of twenty. The census taken in 1890 shows that these twenty slaves had increased to 7,638,360. About 6,353,341 of this

number were residing in the Southern
States, and 1,283,029 were scattered
throughout the Northern and Western
States. I think I am pretty safe in
predicting that the census to be taken
in 1900 will show that there are not far
from ten millions of people of African
descent in the United States. The
great majority of these, of course, reside in the Southern States. The problem is how to make these millions
of Negroes self-supporting, intelligent,
economical and valuable citizens, as
well as how to bring about proper relations between them and the white citizens among whom they live. This is
the question upon which I shall try to
throw some light in the chapters which
follow.

When the Negroes were first brought
to America, they were owned by white
people in all sections of this country, as
is well known,— in the New England,
the Middle, and in the Southern States.

It was soon found, however, that slave labour was not remunerative in the Northern States, and for that reason by far the greater proportion of the slaves were held in the Southern States, where their labour in raising cotton, rice, and sugar-cane was more productive. The growth of the slave population in America was constant and rapid. Beginning, as I have stated, with fourteen, in 1619, the number increased at such a rate that the total number of Negroes in America in 1800 was 1,001,463. This number increased by 1860 to 3,950,000. A few people predicted that freedom would result disastrously to the Negro, as far as numerical increase was concerned; but so far the census figures have failed to bear out this prediction. On the other hand, the census of 1890 shows that the Negro population had increased from 3,950,000 in 1860 to 7,638,260 twenty-five years after the war. It is my opinion that the rate of increase in the future will be still greater than it has been from the close of the war of the Rebellion up to the present time, for the reason that the very sudden changes which took place in the life of the Negro, because of having his freedom, plunged him into many excesses that were detrimental to his physical well-being. Of course, freedom found him unprepared in clothing, in shelter and in knowledge of how to care for his body. During slavery the slave mother had little control of her own children, and did not therefore have the practice and experience of rearing children in a suitable manner. Now that the Negro is being taught in thousands of schools how to take care of his body, and in thousands of homes mothers are learning how to control their children, I believe that the rate of increase, as I have stated, will be still greater than it has been in the past. In too many cases the Negro had the idea that freedom meant merely license to do as he pleased, to work or not to work; but this erroneous idea is more and more disappearing, by reason of the education in the right direction which the Negro is constantly receiving.

During the four years that the Civil War lasted, the greater proportion of the Negroes remained in the South, and worked faithfully for the support of their masters' families, who, as a general rule, were away in the war. The self-control which the Negro exhibited during the war marks, it seems to me, one of the most important chapters in the history of the race. Notwithstanding he knew that his master was away from home, fighting a battle which, if successful, would result in his continued enslavement, yet he worked faithfully for the support of the master's family. If the Negro had yielded to the temptation and suggestion to use the torch or dagger in an attempt to destroy his

8

master's property and family, the result would have been that the war would have been ended quickly; for the master would have returned from the battle-field to protect and defend his property and family. But the Negro to the last was faithful to the trust that had been thrust upon him, and during the four years of war in which the male members of the family were absent from their homes there is not a single instance recorded where he in any way attempted to outrage the family of the master or in any way to injure his property.

Not only is this true, but all through the years of preparation for the war and during the war itself the Negro showed himself to be an uncompromising friend to the Union. In fact, of all the charges brought against him, there is scarcely a single instance where one has been charged with being a traitor to his country. This has been true whether he has been in a state of slavery or in a state of freedom.

From 1865 to 1876 constituted what perhaps may be termed the days of Reconstruction. This was the period when the Southern States which had withdrawn from the Union were making an effort to reinstate themselves and to establish a permanent system of State government. At the close of the war both the Southern white man and the Negro found themselves in the midst of poverty. The ex-master returned from the war to find his slave property gone, his farms and other industries in a state of collapse, and the whole industrial or economic system upon which he had depended for years entirely disorganised. As we review calmly and dispassionately the period of reconstruction, we must use a great deal of sympathy and generosity. The weak point, to my mind, in the reconstruction era was that no strong force was brought to bear in the

direction of preparing the Negro to
become an intelligent, reliable citizen
and voter. The main effort seems to
have been in the direction of controlling
his vote for the time being, regardless
of future interests. I hardly believe
that any race of people with similar
preparation and similar surroundings
would have acted more wisely or very
differently from the way the Negro
acted during the period of reconstruction.

Without experience, without preparation, and in most cases without ordinary intelligence, he was encouraged to
leave the field and shop and enter politics. That under such circumstances
he should have made mistakes is very
natural. I do not believe that the
Negro was so much at fault for entering so largely into politics, and for the
mistakes that were made in too many
cases, as were the unscrupulous white
leaders who got the Negro's confidence

and controlled his vote to further their
own ends, regardless, in many cases, of
the permanent welfare of the Negro. I
have always considered it unfortunate
that the Southern white man did not
make more of an effort during the period
of reconstruction to get the confidence
and sympathy of the Negro, and thus
have been able to keep him in close
touch and sympathy in politics. It was
also unfortunate that the Negro was so
completely alienated from the Southern
white man in all political matters. I
think it would have been better for all
concerned if, immediately after the close
of the war, an educational and property
qualification for the exercise of the franchise had been prescribed that would
have applied fairly and squarely to both
races; and, also, if, in educating the
Negro, greater stress had been put
upon training him along the lines of
industry for which his services were
in the greatest demand in the South.

In a word, too much stress was placed upon the mere matter of voting and holding political office rather than upon the preparation for the highest citizenship. In saying what I have, I do not mean to convey the impression that the whole period of reconstruction was barren of fruitful results. While it is not a very encouraging chapter in the history of our country, I believe that this period did serve to point out many weak points in our effort to elevate the Negro, and that we are now taking advantage of the mistakes that were made. The period of reconstruction served at least to show the world that with proper preparation and with a sufficient foundation the Negro possesses the elements out of which men of the highest character and usefulness can be developed. I might name several characters who were brought before the world by reason of the reconstruction period. I give one as an example

of others: Hon. Blanche K. Bruce, who
had been a slave, but who held many
honourable positions in the State of
Mississippi, including an election to the
United States Senate, where he served
a full term; later he was twice appointed Register of the United States
Treasury. In all these positions Mr.
Bruce gave the greatest satisfaction,
and not a single whisper of dishonesty
or incompetency has ever been heard
against him. During the period of his
public life he was brought into active
and daily contact with Northern and
Southern white people, all of whom
speak of him in the highest measure
of respect and confidence.

What the Negro wants and what the
country wants to do is to take advantage of all the lessons that were taught
during the days of reconstruction, and
apply these lessons bravely, honestly,
in laying the foundation upon which
the Negro can stand in the future and

make himself a useful, honourable, and desirable citizen, whether he has his residence in the North, the South, or the West.

CHAPTER II.

In order that the reader may understand me and why I lay so much stress upon the importance of pushing the doctrine of industrial education for the Negro, it is necessary, first of all, to review the condition of affairs at the present time in the Southern States. For years I have had something of an opportunity to study the Negro at first-hand; and I feel that I know him pretty well,— him and his needs, his failures and his successes, his desires and the likelihood of their fulfilment. I have studied him and his relations with his white neighbours, and striven to find how these relations may be made more conducive to the general peace and welfare both of the South and of the country at large.

In the Southern part of the United States there are twenty-two millions of people who are bound to the fifty millions of the North by ties which neither

can tear asunder if they would. The
most intelligent in a New York community has his intelligence darkened
by the ignorance of a fellow-citizen in
the Mississippi bottoms. The most
wealthy in New York City would be
more wealthy but for the poverty of
a fellow-being in the Carolina rice
swamps. The most moral and religious men in Massachusetts have their
religion and morality modified by the
degradation of the man in the South
whose religion is a mere matter of form
or of emotionalism. The vote of the
man in Maine that is cast for the highest and purest form of government is
largely neutralised by the vote of the
man in Louisiana whose ballot is stolen
or cast in ignorance. Therefore, when
the South is ignorant, the North is ignorant; when the South is poor, the
North is poor; when the South commits crime, the nation commits crime.
For the citizens of the North there is

no escape; they must help raise the
character of the civilisation in the
South, or theirs will be lowered. No
member of the white race in any part of
the country can harm the weakest or
meanest member of the black race
without the proudest and bluest blood
of the nation being degraded.

It seems to me that there never was
a time in the history of the country
when those interested in education
should the more earnestly consider to
what extent the mere acquiring of the
ability to read and write, the mere ac-
quisition of a knowledge of literature
and science, makes men producers, lovers
of labour, independent, honest, unselfish,
and, above all, good. Call education by
what name you please, if it fails to
bring about these results among the
masses, it falls short of its highest end.
The science, the art, the literature, that
fails to reach down and bring the humblest up to the enjoyment of the fullest

blessings of our government, is weak, no matter how costly the buildings or apparatus used or how modern the methods of instruction employed. The study of arithmetic that does not result in making men conscientious in receiving and counting the ballots of their fellow-men is faulty. The study of art that does not result in making the strong less willing to oppress the weak means little. How I wish that from the most cultured and highly endowed university in the great North to the humblest log cabin school-house in Alabama, we could burn, as it were, into the hearts and heads of all that usefulness, that service to our brother, is the supreme end of education. Putting the thought more directly as it applies to conditions in the South, can you make the intelligence of the North affect the South in the same ratio that the ignorance of the South affects the North? Let us take a not improbable case: A great national case is to be decided, one that involves peace or war, the honour or dishonour of our nation,— yea, the very existence of the government. The North and West are divided. There are five million votes to be cast in the South; and, of this number, one-half are ignorant. Not only are one-half the voters ignorant; but, because of the ignorant votes they cast, corruption and dishonesty in a dozen forms have crept into the exercise of the political franchise to such an extent that the conscience of the intelligent class is seared in its attempts to defeat the will of the ignorant voters. Here, then, you have on the one hand an ignorant vote, on the other an intelligent vote minus a conscience. The time may not be far off when to this kind of jury we shall have to look for the votes which shall decide in a large measure the destiny of our democratic institutions.

When a great national calamity stares

us in the face, we are, I fear, too much given to depending on a short "campaign of education" to do on the hustings what should have been accomplished in the school.

With this idea in view, let us examine with more care the condition of civilisation in the South, and the work to be done there before all classes will be fit for the high duties of citizenship. In reference to the Negro race, I am confronted with some embarrassment at the outset, because of the various and conflicting opinions as to what is to be its final place in our economic and political life.

Within the last thirty years — and, I might add, within the last three months,—it has been proven by eminent authority that the Negro is increasing in numbers so fast that it is only a question of a few years before he will far outnumber the white race in the South, and it has also been proven that the

Negro is fast dying out, and it is only a question of a few years before he will have completely disappeared. It has also been proven that education helps the Negro and that education hurts him, that he is fast leaving the South and taking up his residence in the North and West, and that his tendency is to drift toward the low lands of the Mississippi bottoms. It has been proven that education unfits the Negro for work and that education makes him more valuable as a labourer, that he is our greatest criminal and that he is our most law-abiding citizen. In the midst of these conflicting opinions, it is hard to hit upon the truth.

But, also, in the midst of this confusion, there are a few things of which I am certain,— things which furnish a basis for thought and action. I know that whether the Negroes are increasing or decreasing, whether they are growing better or worse, whether they

are valuable or valueless, that a few
years ago some fourteen of them were
brought into this country, and that now
those fourteen are nearly ten millions.
I know that, whether in slavery or freedom, they have always been loyal to the
Stars and Stripes, that no school-house
has been opened for them that has not
been filled, that the 2,000,000 ballots that
they have the right to cast are as potent
for weal or woe as an equal number
cast by the wisest and most influential
men in America. I know that wherever Negro life touches the life of the
nation it helps or it hinders, that
wherever the life of the white race
touches the black it makes it stronger
or weaker. Further, I know that almost every other race that has tried to
look the white man in the face has disappeared. I know, despite all the conflicting opinions, and with a full knowledge of all the Negroes' weaknesses,
that only a few centuries ago they went

into slavery in this country pagans,
that they came out Christians; they
went into slavery as so much property,
they came out American citizens; they
went into slavery without a language,
they came out speaking the proud
Anglo-Saxon tongue; they went into
slavery with the chains clanking about
their wrists, they came out with the
American ballot in their hands.

I submit it to the candid and sober
judgment of all men, if a race that is
capable of such a test, such a transfor-
mation, is not worth saving and making
a part, in reality as well as in name, of
our democratic government. That the
Negro may be fitted for the fullest enjoyment of the privileges and responsibilities of our citizenship, it is important
that the nation be honest and candid
with him, whether honesty and candour
for the time being pleases or displeases
him. It is with an ignorant race as it
is with a child: it craves at first the

superficial, the ornamental signs of progress rather than the reality. The ignorant race is tempted to jump, at one bound, to the position that it has required years of hard struggle for others to reach.

It seems to me that, as a general thing, the temptation in the past in educational and missionary work has been to do for the new people that which was done a thousand years ago, or that which is being done for a people a thousand miles away, without making a careful study of the needs and conditions of the people whom it is designed to help. The temptation is to run all people through a certain educational mould, regardless of the condition of the subject or the end to be accomplished. This has been the case too often in the South in the past, I am sure. Men have tried to use, with these simple people just freed from slavery and with no past, no inherited traditions

of learning, the same methods of education which they have used in New England, with all its inherited traditions and
desires. The Negro is behind the white
man because he has not had the same
chance, and not from any inherent difference in his nature and desires. What
the race accomplishes in these first fifty
years of freedom will at the end of these
years, in a large measure, constitute its
past. It is, indeed, a responsibility that
rests upon this nation,— the foundation
laying for a people of its past, present,
and future at one and the same time.

One of the weakest points in connection with the present development of
the race is that so many get the idea
that the mere filling of the head with
a knowledge of mathematics, the sciences, and literature, means success in
life. Let it be understood, in every
corner of the South, among the Negro
youth at least, that knowledge will
benefit little except as it is harnessed,

except as its power is pointed in a direction that will bear upon the present needs and condition of the race. There is in the heads of the Negro youth of the South enough general and floating knowledge of chemistry, of botany, of zoölogy, of geology, of mechanics, of electricity, of mathematics, to reconstruct and develop a large part of the agricultural, mechanical, and domestic life of the race. But how much of it is brought to a focus along lines of practical work? In cities of the South like Atlanta, how many coloured mechanical engineers are there? or how many machinists? how many civil engineers? how many architects? how many house decorators? In the whole State of Georgia, where eighty per cent. of the coloured people depend upon agriculture, how many men are there who are well grounded in the principles and practices of scientific farming? or dairy work? or fruit culture? or floriculture?

For example, not very long ago I had a conversation with a young coloured man who is a graduate of one of the prominent universities of this country. The father of this man is comparatively ignorant, but by hard work and the exercise of common sense he has become the owner of two thousand acres of land. He owns more than a score of horses, cows, and mules and swine in large numbers, and is considered a prosperous farmer. In college the son of this farmer has studied chemistry, botany, zoölogy, surveying, and political economy. In my conversation I asked this young man how many acres his father cultivated in cotton and how many in corn. With a far-off gaze up into the heavens he answered that he did not know. When I asked him the classification of the soils on his father's farm, he did not know. He did not know how many horses or cows his father owned nor of what breeds they were, and seemed surprised that he should be asked such questions. It never seemed to have entered his mind that on his father's farm was the place to make his chemistry, his mathematics, and his literature penetrate and reflect itself in every acre of land, every bushel of corn, every cow, and every pig.

Let me give other examples of this mistaken sort of education. When a mere boy, I saw a young coloured man, who had spent several years in school, sitting in a common cabin in the South, studying a French grammar. I noted the poverty, the untidiness, the want of system and thrift, that existed about the cabin, notwithstanding his knowledge of French and other academic studies.

Again, not long ago I saw a coloured minister preparing his Sunday sermon just as the New England minister prepares his sermon. But this coloured minister was in a broken-down, leaky, rented log cabin, with weeds in the yard, surrounded by evidences of poverty, filth, and want of thrift. This minister had spent some time in school studying theology. How much better it would have been to have had this minister taught the dignity of labour, taught theoretical and practical farming in connection with his theology, so that he could have added to his meagre salary, and set an example for his people in the matter of living in a decent house, and having a knowledge of correct farming! In a word, this minister should have been taught that his condition, and that of his people, was not that of a New England community; and he should have been so trained as to meet the actual needs and conditions of the coloured people in this community, so that a foundation might be laid that would, in the future, make a community like New England communities.

Since the Civil War, no one object has been more misunderstood than that of the object and value of industrial education for the Negro. To begin with, it must be borne in mind that the condition that existed in the South immediately after the war, and that now exists, is a peculiar one, without a parallel in history. This being true, it seems to me that the wise and honest thing to do is to make a study of the actual condition and environment of the Negro, and do that which is best for him, regardless of whether the same thing has been done for another race in exactly the same way. There are those among the white race and those among the black race who assert, with a good deal of earnestness, that there is no difference between the white man and the black man in this country. This sounds very pleasant and tickles the fancy; but, when the test of hard, cold logic is applied to it, it must be acknowledged that there is a difference,— not an inherent one, not a racial one, but a difference growing out of unequal opportunities in the past.

If I may be permitted to criticise the educational work that has been done in the South, I would say that the weak point has been in the failure to recognise this difference.

Negro education, immediately after the war in most cases, was begun too nearly at the point where New England education had ended. Let me illustrate. One of the saddest sights I ever saw was the placing of a three hundred dollar rosewood piano in a country school in the South that was located in the midst of the " Black Belt." Am I arguing against the teaching of instrumental music to the Negroes in that community? Not at all; only I should have deferred those music lessons about twenty-five years. There are numbers of such pianos in thousands of New England homes. But behind the piano in the New England home there are one hundred years of toil, sacrifice, and economy; there is the small manufacturing industry, started several years ago by hand power, now grown into a great business; there is ownership in land, a comfortable home, free from debt, and a bank account. In this "Black Belt" community where this piano went, four-fifths of the people owned no land, many lived in rented one-room cabins, many were in debt for food supplies, many mortgaged their crops for the food on which to live, and not one had a bank account. In this case, how much wiser it would have been to have taught the girls in this community sewing, intelligent and economical cooking, housekeeping, something of dairying and horticulture? The boys should have been taught something of farming in connection with their common-school education, instead of awakening in them a desire for a musical instrument which resulted in their parents going into debt

33

for a third-rate piano or organ before a home was purchased. Industrial lessons would have awakened, in this community, a desire for homes, and would have given the people the ability to free themselves from industrial slavery to the extent that most of them would have soon purchased homes. After the home and the necessaries of life were supplied could come the piano. One piano lesson in a home of one's own is worth twenty in a rented log cabin.

All that I have just written, and the various examples illustrating it, show the present helpless condition of my people in the South,— how fearfully they lack the primary training for good living and good citizenship, how much they stand in need of a solid foundation on which to build their future success. I believe, as I have many times said in my various addresses in the North and in the South, that the main reason for the existence of this curious state of affairs is the lack of practical training in the ways of life.

There is, too, a great lack of money with which to carry on the educational work in the South. I was in a county in a Southern State not long ago where there are some thirty thousand coloured people and about seven thousand whites. In this county not a single public school for Negroes had been open that year longer than three months, not a single coloured teacher had been paid more than $15 per month for his teaching. Not one of these schools was taught in a building that was worthy of the name of school-house. In this county the State or public authorities do not own a single dollar's worth of school property,— not a school-house, a blackboard, or a piece of crayon. Each coloured child had had spent on him that year for his education about fifty cents, while each child in New York or Massachusetts had had spent on him that year for education not far from $20. And yet each citizen of this county is expected to share the burdens and privileges of our democratic form of government just as intelligently and conscientiously as the citizens of New York or Boston. A vote in this county means as much to the nation as a vote in the city of Boston. Crime in this county is as truly an arrow aimed at the heart of the government as a crime committed in the streets of Boston.

A single school-house built this year in a town near Boston to shelter about three hundred pupils cost more for building alone than is spent yearly for the education, including buildings, apparatus, teachers, for the whole coloured school population of Alabama. The Commissioner of Education for the State of Georgia not long ago reported to the State legislature that in that State there were two hundred thousand children that had entered no school the

year past and one hundred thousand
more who were at school but a few
days, making practically three hundred
thousand children between six and
eighteen years of age that are growing
up in ignorance in one Southern State
alone. The same report stated that
outside of the cities and towns, while
the average number of school-houses
in a county was sixty, all of these
sixty school-houses were worth in lump
less than $2,000, and the report further
added that many of the school-houses
in Georgia were not fit for horse stables.
I am glad to say, however, that vast improvement over this condition is being made in Georgia under the inspired
leadership of State Commissioner Glenn,
and in Alabama under the no less zeal-
ous leadership of Commissioner Aber-
crombie.

These illustrations, so far as they
concern the Gulf States, are not exceptional cases ; nor are they overdrawn.

The Future of the American Negro

Until there is industrial independence, it is hardly possible to have good living and a pure ballot in the country districts. In these States it is safe to say that not more than one black man in twenty owns the land he cultivates. Where so large a proportion of a people are dependent, live in other people's houses, eat other people's food, and wear clothes they have not paid for, it is pretty hard to expect them to live fairly and vote honestly.

I have thus far referred mainly to the Negro race. But there is another side. The longer I live and the more I study the question, the more I am convinced that it is not so much a problem as to what the white man will do with the Negro as what the Negro will do with the white man and his civilisation. In considering this side of the subject, I thank God that I have grown to the point where I can sympathise with a white man as much as I can sympathise with a black man. I have grown to the point where I can sympathise with a Southern white man as much as I can sympathise with a Northern white man.

As bearing upon the future of our civilisation, I ask of the North what of their white brethren in the South,— those who have suffered and are still suffering the consequences of American slavery, for which both North and South were responsible? Those of the great and prosperous North still owe to their less fortunate brethren of the Caucasian race in the South, not less than to themselves, a serious and uncompleted duty. What was the task the North asked the South to perform? Returning to their destitute homes after years of war to face blasted hopes, devastation, a shattered industrial system, they asked them to add to their own burdens that of preparing in education, politics, and economics, in a few short years, for citizenship, four millions of former slaves. That the South, staggering under the burden, made blunders, and that in a measure there has been disappointment, no one need be surprised. The educators, the statesmen, the philanthropists, have imperfectly comprehended their duty toward the millions of poor whites in the South who were buffeted for two hundred years between slavery and freedom, between civilisation and degradation, who were disregarded by both master and slave. It needs no prophet to tell the character of our future civilisation when the poor white boy in the country districts of the South receives one dollar's worth of education and the boy of the same class in the North twenty dollars' worth, when one never enters a reading-room or library and the other has reading-rooms and libraries in every ward and town, when one hears lectures and sermons once in two months and the other can hear a lecture or a sermon every day in the year.

The time has come, it seems to me, when in this matter we should rise above party or race or sectionalism into the region of duty of man to man, of citizen to citizen, of Christian to Christian; and if the Negro, who has been oppressed and denied his rights in a Christian land, can help the whites of the North and South to rise, can be the inspiration of their rising, into this atmosphere of generous Christian brotherhood and self-forgetfulness, he will see in it a recompense for all that he has suffered in the past.

CHAPTER III.

In the heart of the Black Belt of the South in *ante-bellum* days there was a large estate, with palatial mansion, surrounded by a beautiful grove, in which grew flowers and shrubbery of every description. Magnificent specimens of animal life grazed in the fields, and in grain and all manner of plant growth this estate was a model. In a word, it was the highest type of the product of slave labor.

Then came the long years of war, then freedom, then the trying years of reconstruction. The master returned from the war to find the faithful slaves who had been the bulwark of this household in possession of their freedom. Then there began that social and industrial revolution in the South which it is hard for any who was not really a part of it to appreciate or understand. Gradually, day by day, this ex-master began

to realise, with a feeling almost inde-
scribable, to what an extent he and his
family had grown to be dependent
upon the activity and faithfulness of
his slaves ; began to appreciate to what
an extent slavery had sapped his sinews
of strength and independence, how his
dependence upon slave labour had deprived him and his offspring of the
benefit of technical and industrial training, and, worst of all, had unconsciously
led him to see in labour drudgery and
degradation instead of beauty, dignity,
and civilising power. At first there
was a halt in this man's life. He
cursed the North and he cursed the
Negro. Then there was despair, almost utter hopelessness, over his weak
and childlike condition. The temptation was to forget all in drink, and to
this temptation there was a gradual
yielding. With the loss of physical
vigour came the loss of mental grasp
and pride in surroundings. There was

the falling off of a piece of plaster from the walls of the house which was not replaced, then another and still another. Gradually, the window-panes began to disappear, then the door-knobs. Touches of paint and whitewash, which once helped to give life, were no more to be seen. The hinges disappeared from the gate, then a board from the fence, then others in quick succession. Weeds and unmown grass covered the once well-kept lawn. Sometimes there were servants for domestic duties, and sometimes there were none. In the absence of servants the unsatisfactory condition of the food told that it was being prepared by hands unschooled to such duties. As the years passed by, debts accumulated in every direction. The education of the children was neglected. Lower and lower sank the industrial, financial, and spiritual condition of the household. For the first time the awful truth of Scripture, "Whatsoever a man soweth, that shall he also reap," seemed to dawn upon him with a reality that it is hard for mortal to appreciate. Within a few months the whole mistake of slavery seemed to have concentrated itself upon this household. And this was one of many.

We have seen how the ending of slavery and the beginning of freedom produced not only a shock, but a standstill, and in many cases a collapse, that lasted several years in the life of many white men. If the sudden change thus affected the white man, should this not teach us that we should have more sympathy than has been shown in many cases with the Negro in connection with his new and changed life? That they made many mistakes, plunged into excesses, undertook responsibilities for which they were not fitted, in many cases took liberty to mean license, is not to be wondered at. It is my opinion that the next forty years are going

to show by many per cent. a higher degree of progress in the life of the Negro
along all lines than has been shown
during the first thirty years of his life.
Certainly, the first thirty years of the
Negro's life was one of experiment; and
consequently, under such conditions, he
was not able to settle down to real,
earnest, hard common sense efforts to
better his condition. While this was
true in a great many cases, on the other
hand a large proportion of the race,
even from the first, saw what was needed
for their new life, and began to settle
down to lead an industrious, frugal existence, and to educate their children
and in every way prepare themselves
for the responsibilities of American
citizenship.

The wonder is that the Negro has
made as few mistakes as he has, when
we consider all the surrounding circumstances. Columns of figures have been
gleaned from the census reports within

the last quarter of a century to show the great amount of crime committed by the Negro in excess of that committed by other races. No one will deny the fact that the proportion of crime by the present generation of Negroes is seriously large, but I believe that any other race with the Negro's history and present environment would have shown about the same criminal record.

Another consideration which we must always bear in mind in considering the Negro is that he had practically no home life in slavery; that is, the mother and father did not have the responsibility, and consequently the experience, of training their own children. The matter of child training was left to the master and mistress. Consequently, it has only been within the last thirty years that the Negro parents have had the actual responsibility and experience of training their own children. That they have made some mistakes in thus training them is not to be wondered at. Many families scattered over all parts of the United States have not yet been able to bring themselves together. When the Negro parents shall have had thirty or forty additional years in which to found homes and get experience in the training of their children, I believe that we will find that the amount of crime will be considerably less than it is now shown to be.

In too large a measure the Negro race began its development at the wrong end, simply because neither white nor black understood the case; and no wonder, for there had never been such a case in the history of the world.

To show where this primary mistake has led in its evil results, I wish to produce some examples showing plainly how prone we have been to make our education formal, superficial, instead of making it meet the needs of conditions.

In order to emphasise the matter
more fully, I repeat, at least eighty per
cent. of the coloured people in the
South are found in the rural districts,
and they are dependent on agriculture
in some form for their support. Notwithstanding that we have practically
a whole race dependent upon agriculture, and notwithstanding that thirty
years have passed since our freedom,
aside from what has been done at
Hampton and Tuskegee and one or two
other institutions, but very little has
been attempted by State or philanthropy
in the way of educating the race in this
one industry upon which its very existence depends. Boys have been taken
from the farms and educated in law,
theology, Hebrew and Greek,— educated in everything else except the very
subject that they should know most
about. I question whether among all
the educated coloured people in the
United States you can find six, if we ex-

cept those from the institutions named, who have received anything like a thorough training in agriculture. It would have seemed that, since self-support, industrial independence, is the first condition for lifting up any race, that education in theoretical and practical agriculture, horticulture, dairying, and stock-raising, should have occupied the first place in our system.

Some time ago, when we decided to make tailoring a part of our training at the Tuskegee Institute, I was amazed to find that it was almost impossible to find in the whole country an educated coloured man who could teach the making of clothing. We could find them by the score who could teach astronomy, theology, grammar, or Latin, but almost none who could instruct in the making of clothing, something that has to be used by every one of us every day in the year. How often has my heart been made to sink as I have gone through

the South and into the homes of people,
and found women who could converse
intelligently on Grecian history, who
had studied geometry, could analyse
the most complex sentences, and yet
could not analyse the poorly cooked
and still more poorly served corn bread
and fat meat that they and their families
were eating three times a day! It is
little trouble to find girls who can locate
Pekin or the Desert of Sahara on an
artificial globe, but seldom can you find
one who can locate on an actual dinner
table the proper place for the carving
knife and fork or the meat and vegetables.

A short time ago, in one of the
Southern cities, a coloured man died
who had received training as a skilled
mechanic during the days of slavery.
Later by his skill and industry he built
up a great business as a house contractor and builder. In this same city
there are 35,000 coloured people, among

them young men who have been well
educated in the languages and in literature; but not a single one could be
found who had been so trained in mechanical and architectural drawing that
he could carry on the business which
this ex-slave had built up, and so it was
soon scattered to the wind. Aside from
the work done in the institutions that
I have mentioned, you can find almost
no coloured men who have been trained
in the principles of architecture, notwithstanding the fact that a vast majority
of our race are without homes. Here,
then, are the three prime conditions for
growth, for civilisation,— food, clothing,
shelter; and yet we have been the slaves
of forms and customs to such an extent
that we have failed in a large measure
to look matters squarely in the face and
meet actual needs.

It may well be asked by one who
has not carefully considered the matter:
" What has become of all those skilled

farm-hands that used to be on the old plantations? Where are those wonderful cooks we hear about, where those exquisitely trained house servants, those cabinet makers, and the jacks-of-all-trades that were the pride of the South?" This is easily answered,— they are mostly dead. The survivors are too old to work. "But did they not train their children?" is the natural question. Alas! the answer is "no." Their skill was so commonplace to them, and to their former masters, that neither thought of it as being a hard-earned or desirable accomplishment: it was natural, like breathing. Their children would have it as a matter of course. What their children needed was education. So they went out into the world, the ambitious ones, and got education, and forgot the necessity of the ordinary training to live.

God for two hundred and fifty years, in my opinion, prepared the way for the redemption of the Negro through industrial development. First, he made the Southern white man do business with the Negro for two hundred and fifty years in a way that no one else has done business with him. If a Southern white man wanted a house or a bridge built, he consulted a Negro mechanic about the plan and about the actual building of the house or bridge. If he wanted a suit of clothes or a pair of shoes made, it was to the Negro tailor or shoemaker that he talked. Secondly, every large slave plantation in the South was, in a limited sense, an industrial school. On these plantations there were scores of young coloured men and women who were constantly being trained, not alone as common farmers, but as carpenters, blacksmiths, wheelwrights, plasterers, brick masons, engineers, bridge-builders, cooks, dressmakers, housekeepers, etc. I would be the last to apologise for the curse of slavery; but I am simply stating facts. This training was crude and was given for selfish purposes, and did not answer the highest ends, because there was the absence of brain training in connection with that of the hand. Nevertheless, this business contact with the Southern white man, and the industrial training received on these plantations, put the Negro at the close of the war into possession of all the common and skilled labour in the South. For nearly twenty years after the war, except in one or two cases, the value of the industrial training given by the Negroes' former masters on the plantations and elsewhere was overlooked. Negro men and women were educated in literature, mathematics, and the sciences, with no thought of what had taken place on these plantations for two and a half centuries. After twenty years, those who were trained as mechanics, etc., during slavery began to disappear by death; and gradually we awoke to the fact that we had no one to take their places. We had scores of young men learned in Greek, but few in carpentry or mechanical or architectural drawing. We had trained many in Latin, but almost none as engineers, bridge-builders, and machinists. Numbers were taken from the farm and educated, but were educated in everything else except agriculture. Hence they had no sympathy with farm life, and did not return to it.

This last that I have been saying is practically a repetition of what I have said in the preceding paragraph; but, to emphasise it,— and this point is one of the most important I wish to impress on the reader,— it is well to repeat, to say the same thing twice. Oh, if only more who had the shaping of the education of the Negro could have, thirty years ago, realised, and made others realise, where the forgetting of the years of manual training and the sudden acquiring of education were going to lead the Negro race, what a saving it would have been! How much less my race would have had to answer for, as well as the white!

But it is too late to cry over what might have been. It is time to make up, as soon as possible, for this mistake, — time for both races to acknowledge it, and go forth on the course that, it seems to me, all must now see to be the right one,— industrial education.

As an example of what a well-trained and educated Negro may now do, and how ready to acknowledge him a Southern white man may be, let me return once more to the plantation I spoke of in the first part of this chapter. As the years went by, the night seemed to grow darker, so that all seemed hopeless and lost. At this point relief and strength came from an unexpected source. This Southern white man's idea of Negro education had been that it merely meant a parrot-like absorption of Anglo-Saxon civilisation, with a special tendency to imitate the weaker elements of the white man's character; that it meant merely the high hat, kid gloves, a showy walking cane, patent leather shoes, and all the rest of it. To this ex-master it seemed impossible that the education of the Negro could produce any other results. And so, last of all, did he expect help or encouragement from an educated black man; but it was just from this source that help came. Soon after the process of decay began in this white man's estate, the education of a certain black man began, and began on a logical, sensible basis. It was an education that would fit him to see and appreciate the physical and moral conditions that existed in his own family and neighbourhood, and, in the present generation, would fit him to apply himself to their relief. By chance this educated Negro strayed into the employ of this white man. His employer soon learned that this Negro not only had a knowledge of science, mathematics, and literature in his head, but in his hands as well. This black man applied his knowledge of agricultural chemistry to the redemption of the soil; and soon the washes and gulleys began to disappear, and the waste places began to bloom. New and improved machinery in a few months began to rob labour of its toil and drudgery. The animals were given systematic and kindly attention. Fences were repaired and rebuilt. Whitewash and paint were made to do duty. Everywhere order slowly began to replace confusion; hope, despair; and profits, losses. As he observed, day by day, new life and strength being imparted to every department of his property, this white son of the South began revising his own creed regarding the wisdom of educating Negroes.

Hitherto his creed regarding the value of an educated Negro had been rather a plain and simple one, and read: "The only end that could be accomplished by educating a black man was to enable him to talk properly to a mule; and the Negro's education did great injustice to the mule, since the language tended to confuse him and make him balky."

We need not continue the story, except to add that to-day the grasp of the hand of this ex-slaveholder, and the listening to his hearty words of gratitude and commendation for the education of the Negro, are enough to compensate those who have given and those who have worked and sacrificed for the elevation of my people through all of these years. If we are patient, wise, unselfish, and courageous, such examples will multiply as the years go by.

Before closing this chapter,— which, I think, has clearly shown that there is at present a very distinct lack of industrial training in the South among the Negroes,— I wish to say a few words in regard to certain objections, or rather misunderstandings, which have from time to time arisen in regard to the matter.

Many have had the thought that industrial training was meant to make the Negro work, much as he worked during the days of slavery. This is far from my idea of it. If this training has any value for the Negro, as it has for the white man, it consists in teaching the Negro how rather not to work, but how to make the forces of nature — air, water, horse-power, steam, and electric power — work for him, how to lift labour up out of toil and drudgery into that which is dignified and beautiful. The Negro in the South works, and he works hard; but his lack of skill, coupled with ignorance, causes him too often to do his work in the most costly and shiftless manner, and this has kept him near the bottom of the ladder in the business world. I repeat that industrial education teaches the Negro how not to drudge in his work. Let him who doubts this contrast the Negro in the South toiling through a field of oats with an old-fashioned reaper with the white man on a modern farm in the West, sitting upon a modern " harvester," behind two spirited horses, with an umbrella over him, using a machine that cuts and binds the oats at the same time,— doing four times as much work as the black man with one half the labour. Let us give the black man so much skill and brains that he can cut oats like the white man, then he can compete with him. The Negro works in cotton, and has no trouble so long as his labour is confined to the lower forms of work,— the planting, the picking, and the ginning; but, when the Negro attempts to follow the bale of cotton up through the higher stages, through the mill where it is made into the finer fabrics, where the larger profit appears, he is told that he is not wanted.

The Negro can work in wood and iron; and no one objects so long as he confines his work to the felling of trees and sawing of boards, to the digging of iron ore and making of pig iron. But, when the Negro attempts to follow this tree into the factory where it is made into desks and chairs and railway coaches, or when he attempts to follow the pig iron into the factory where it is. made into knife-blades and watch-springs, the Negro's trouble begins. And what is the objection? Simply that the Negro lacks the skill, coupled with brains, necessary to compete with the white man, or that, when white men refuse to work with coloured men, enough skilled and educated coloured men cannot be found able to superintend and man every part of any one large industry; and hence, for these reasons, they are constantly being barred out. The Negro must become, in a larger measure, an intelligent producer as well as a consumer. There should be a more vital and practical connection between the Negro's educated brain and his opportunity of earning his daily living.

A very weak argument often used against pushing industrial training for the Negro is that the Southern white man favours it, and, therefore, it is not best for the Negro. Although I was born a slave, I am thankful that I am able so far to rid myself of prejudice as to be able to accept a good thing, whether it comes from a black man or a white man, a Southern man or a Northern man. Industrial education will not only help the Negro directly in the matter of industrial development, but also in bringing about more satisfactory relations between him and the Southern white man. For the sake of the Negro

64

and the Southern white man there are many things in the relation of the two races that must soon be changed. We cannot depend wholly upon abuse or condemnation of the Southern white man to bring about these changes. Each race must be educated to see matters in a broad, high, generous, Christian spirit: we must bring the two races together, not estrange them. The Negro must live for all time by the side of the Southern white man. The man is unwise who does not cultivate in every manly way the friendship and good will of his next-door neighbour, whether he be black or white. I repeat that industrial training will help cement the friendship of the two races. The history of the world proves that trade, commerce, is the forerunner of peace and civilisation as between races and nations. The Jew, who was once in about the same position that the Negro is to-day, has now recognition, because he has entwined himself about America in a business and industrial sense. Say or think what we will, it is the tangible or visible element that is going to tell largely during the next twenty years in the solution of the race problem.

CHAPTER IV.

ONE of the main problems as regards the education of the Negro is how to have him use his education to the best advantage after he has secured it. In saying this, I do not want to be understood as implying that the problem of simple ignorance among the masses has been settled in the South; for this is far from true. The amount of ignorance still prevailing among the Negroes, especially in the rural districts, is very large and serious. But I repeat, we must go farther if we would secure the best results and most gratifying returns in public good for the money spent than merely to put academic education in the Negro's head with the idea that this will settle everything.

In his present condition it is important, in seeking after what he terms the ideal, that the Negro should not neglect to prepare himself to take advantage of the opportunities that are right about his door. If he lets these opportunities slip, I fear they will never be his again. In saying this, I mean always that the Negro should have the most thorough mental and religious training; for without it no race can succeed. Because of his past history and environment and present condition it is important that he be carefully guided for years to come in the proper use of his education. Much valuable time has been lost and money spent in vain, because too many have not been educated with the idea of fitting them to do well the things which they could get to do. Because of the lack of proper direction of the Negro's education, some good friends of his, North and South, have not taken that interest in it that they otherwise would have taken. In too many cases where merely literary education alone has been given the Negro youth, it has resulted in an exaggerated estimate of his importance in the world, and an increase of wants which his education has not fitted him to supply.

But, in discussing this subject, one is often met with the question, Should not the Negro be encouraged to prepare himself for any station in life that any other race fills? I would say, Yes; but the surest way for the Negro to reach the highest positions is to prepare himself to fill well at the present time the basic occupations. This will give him a foundation upon which to stand while securing what is called the more exalted positions. The Negro has the right to study law; but success will come to the race sooner if it produces intelligent, thrifty farmers, mechanics, and housekeepers to support the lawyers. The want of proper direction of the use of the Negro's education results in tempting too many to live mainly by their wits, without producing anything that is of real value to the world. Let me quote examples of this.

Hayti, Santo Domingo, and Liberia, although among the richest countries in natural resources in the world, are discouraging examples of what must happen to any people who lack industrial or technical training. It is said that in Liberia there are no wagons, wheelbarrows, or public roads, showing very plainly that there is a painful absence of public spirit and thrift. What is true of Liberia is also true in a measure of the republics of Hayti and Santo Domingo. The people have not yet learned the lesson of turning their education toward the cultivation of the soil and the making of the simplest implements for agricultural and other forms of labour.

Much would have been done toward laying a sound foundation for general prosperity if some attention had been spent in this direction. General education itself has no bearing on the subject at issue, because, while there is no well-established public school system in either of these countries, yet large numbers of men of both Hayti and Santo Domingo have been educated in France for generations. This is especially true of Hayti. The education has been altogether in the direction of *belles lettres*, however, and practically little in the direction of industrial and scientific education.

It is a matter of common knowledge that Hayti has to send abroad even to secure engineers for her men-of-war, for plans for her bridges and other work requiring technical knowledge and skill. I should very much regret to see any such condition obtain in any large measure as regards the coloured people in the South, and yet this will be our fate if industrial education is much longer neglected. We have spent much time in the South in educating men and women in letters alone, too, and must now turn our attention more than ever toward educating them so as to supply their wants and needs. It is more lamentable to see educated people unable to support themselves than to see uneducated people in the same condition. Ambition all along this line must be stimulated.

If educated men and women of the race will see and acknowledge the necessity of practical industrial training and go to work with a zeal and determination, their example will be followed by others, who are now without ambition of any kind.

The race cannot hope to come into its own until the young coloured men and women make up their minds to assist in the general development along these lines. The elder men and women trained in the hard school of slavery, and who so long possessed all of the labour, skilled and unskilled, of the South, are dying out; their places must be filled by their children, or we shall lose our hold upon these occupations. Leaders in these occupations are needed now more than ever.

It is not enough that the idea be inculcated that coloured people should get book learning; along with it they should be taught that book education and industrial development must go hand in hand. No race which fails to do this can ever hope to succeed. Phillips Brooks gave expression to the sentiment: "One generation gathers the material, and the next generation builds the palaces." As I understand it, he wished to inculcate the idea that one generation lays the foundation for succeeding generations. The rough affairs of life very largely fall to the earlier generation, while the next one has the privilege of dealing with the higher and more æsthetic things of life. This is true of all generations, of all peoples; and, unless the foundation is deeply laid, it is impossible for the succeeding one to have a career in any way approaching success. As regards the coloured men of the South, as regards the coloured men of the United States, this is the generation which, in a large measure, must gather the material with which to lay the foundation for future success.

Some time ago it was my misfortune to see a Negro sixty-five years old living in poverty and filth. I was disgusted, and said to him, "If you are worthy of your freedom, you would surely have changed your condition during the thirty years of freedom which you have enjoyed." He answered: "I do want to change. I want to do something for my wife and children; but I do not know how,— I do not know what to do." I looked into his lean and haggard face, and realised more deeply than ever before the absolute need of captains of industry among the great masses of the coloured people.

It is possible for a race or an individual to have mental development and yet be so handicapped by custom, prejudice, and lack of employment as to dwarf and discourage the whole life. This is the condition that prevails among the race in many of the large cities of the North; and it is to prevent this same condition in the South that I plead with all the earnestness of my heart. Mental development alone will not give us what we want, but mental development tied to hand and heart training will be the salvation of the Negro.

In many respects the next twenty years are going to be the most serious in the history of the race. Within this period it will be largely decided whether the Negro will be able to retain the hold which he now has upon the industries of the South or whether his place will be filled by white people from a distance. The only way he can prevent the industrial occupations slipping from him in all parts of the South, as they have already in certain parts, is for all educators, ministers, and friends of the race to unite in pushing forward in a whole-souled manner the industrial or business development of the Negro, whether in school or out of school. Four times as many young men and women of the race should be receiving industrial training. Just now the Negro is in a position to feel and appreciate the need of this in a way that no one else can. No one can fully appreciate what I am saying who has not walked the streets of a Northern city day after day seeking employment, only to find every door closed against him on account of his colour, except in menial service. It is to prevent the same thing taking place in the South that I plead. We may argue that mental development will take care of all this. Mental development is a good thing. Gold is also a good thing, but gold is worthless without an opportunity to make itself touch the world of trade. Education increases greatly an individual's wants. It is cruel in many cases to increase the wants of the black youth by mental development alone without, at the same time, increasing his ability to supply these increased wants in occupations in which he can find employment.

The place made vacant by the death of the old coloured man who was trained as a carpenter during slavery, and who since the war had been the leading contractor and builder in the Southern town, had to be filled. No young coloured carpenter capable of filling his place could be found. The result was that his place was filled by a white mechanic from the North, or from Europe, or from elsewhere. What is true of carpentry and house-building in this case is true, in a degree, in every skilled occupation; and it is becoming true of common labour. I do not mean to say that all of

the skilled labour has been taken out of
the Negro's hands; but I do mean to say
that in no part of the South is he so
strong in the matter of skilled labour as
he was twenty years ago, except possibly
in the country districts and the smaller
towns. In the more northern of the
Southern cities, such as Richmond and
Baltimore, the change is most apparent;
and it is being felt in every Southern city.
Wherever the Negro has lost ground in-
dustrially in the South, it is not because
there is prejudice against him as a skilled
labourer on the part of the native Southern white man; the Southern white
man generally prefers to do business with
the Negro mechanic rather than with a
white one, because he is accustomed to
do business with the Negro in this respect. There is almost no prejudice
against the Negro in the South in matters of business, so far as the native
whites are concerned; and here is the
entering wedge for the solution of the

race problem. But too often, where the white mechanic or factory operative from the North gets a hold, the trades-union soon follows, and the Negro is crowded to the wall.

But what is the remedy for this condition? First, it is most important that the Negro and his white friends honestly face the facts as they are; otherwise the time will not be very far distant when the Negro of the South will be crowded to the ragged edge of industrial life as he is in the North. There is still time to repair the damage and to reclaim what we have lost.

I stated in the beginning that industrial education for the Negro has been misunderstood. This has been chiefly because some have gotten the idea that industrial development was opposed to the Negro's higher mental development. This has little or nothing to do with the subject under discussion; we should no longer permit such an idea to aid in depriving the Negro of the legacy in the form of skilled labour that was purchased by his forefathers at the price of two hundred and fifty years of slavery. I would say to the black boy what I would say to the white boy, Get all the mental development that your time and pocket-book will allow of,— the more, the better; but the time has come when a larger proportion — not all, for we need professional men and women — of the educated coloured men and women should give themselves to industrial or business life. The professional class will be helped in so far as the rank and file have an industrial foundation, so that they can pay for professional service. Whether they receive the training of the hand while pursuing their academic training or after their academic training is finished, or whether they will get their literary training in an industrial school or college, are questions which each individual must decide for himself. No matter how or where educated, the educated men and women must come to the rescue of the race in the effort to get and hold its industrial footing. I would not have the standard of mental development lowered one whit; for, with the Negro, as with all races, mental strength is the basis of all progress. But I would have a large measure of this mental strength reach the Negroes' actual needs through the medium of the hand. Just now the need is not so much for the common carpenters, brick masons, farmers, and laundry women as for industrial leaders who, in addition to their practical knowledge, can draw plans, make estimates, take contracts; those who understand the latest methods of truck-gardening and the science underlying practical agriculture; those who understand machinery to the extent that they can operate steam and electric laundries, so that our women can hold on to the laundry work in the

South, that is so fast drifting into the hands of others in the large cities and towns.

Having tried to show in previous chapters to what a condition the lack of practical training has brought matters in the South, and by the examples in this chapter where this state of things may go if allowed to run its course, I wish now to show what practical training, even in its infancy among us, has already accomplished.

I noticed, when I first went to Tuskegee to start the Tuskegee Normal and Industrial Institute, that some of the white people about there rather looked doubtfully at me; and I thought I could get their influence by telling them how much algebra and history and science and all those things I had in my head, but they treated me about the same as they did before. They didn't seem to care about the algebra, history, and science that were in my head only.

Those people never even began to have confidence in me until we commenced to build a large three-story brick building, and then another and another, until now we have forty buildings which have been erected largely by the labour of our students; and to-day we have the respect and confidence of all the white people in that section.

There is an unmistakable influence that comes over a white man when he sees a black man living in a two-story brick house that has been paid for. I need not stop to explain. It is the tangible evidence of prosperity. You know Thomas doubted the Saviour after he had risen from the dead; and the Lord said to Thomas, "Reach hither thy finger, and behold my hands; and reach hither thy hand, and thrust it into my side." The tangible evidence convinced Thomas.

We began, soon after going to Tuskegee, the manufacture of bricks. We also started a wheelwright establishment and the manufacture of good wagons and buggies; and the white people came to our institution for that kind of work. We also put in a printing plant, and did job printing for the white people as well as for the blacks.

By having something that these people wanted, we came into contact with them, and our interest became interlinked with their interest, until to-day we have no warmer friends anywhere in the country than we have among the white people of Tuskegee. We have found by experience that the best way to get on well with people is to have something that they want, and that is why we emphasise this Christian Industrial Education.

Not long ago I heard a conversation among three white men something like this. Two of them were berating the Negro, saying the Negro was shiftless and lazy, and all that sort of thing.

The third man listened to their remarks for some time in silence, and then he said: "I don't know what your experience has been; but there is a 'nigger' down our way who owns a good house and lot with about fifty acres of ground. His house is well furnished, and he has got some splendid horses and cattle. He is intelligent and has a bank account. I don't know how the 'niggers' are in your community, but Tobe Jones is a gentleman. Once, when I was hard up, I went to Tobe Jones and borrowed fifty dollars; and he hasn't asked me for it yet. I don't know what kind of 'niggers' you have down your way, but Tobe Jones is a gentleman."

Now what we want to do is to multiply and place in every community these Tobe Joneses; and, just in so far as we can place them throughout the South this race question will disappear.

Suppose there was a black man who had business for the railroads to the amount of ten thousand dollars a year. Do you suppose that, when that black man takes his family aboard the train, they are going to put him into a Jim Crow car and run the risk of losing that ten thousand dollars a year? No, they will put on a Pullman palace car for him.

Some time ago a certain coloured man was passing through the streets of one of the little Southern towns, and he chanced to meet two white men on the street. It happened that this coloured man owns two or three houses and lots, has a good education and a comfortable bank account. One of the white men turned to the other, and said: " By Gosh! It is all I can do to keep from calling that 'nigger' Mister." That's the point we want to get to.

Nothing else so soon brings about right relations between the two races in the South as the commercial progress of the Negro. Friction between the races

will pass away as the black man, by
reason of his skill, intelligence, and
character, can produce something that
the white man wants or respects in the
commercial world. This is another reason why at Tuskegee we push industrial
training. We find that as every year
we put into a Southern community coloured men who can start a brickyard,
a saw-mill, a tin-shop, or a printing-
office,— men who produce something
that makes the white man partly dependent upon the Negro instead of all
the dependence being on the other side,
— a change for the better takes place
in the relations of the races. It is
through the dairy farm, the truck-
garden, the trades, the commercial life,
largely, that the Negro is to find his
way to respect and confidence.

What is the permanent value of the
Hampton and Tuskegee system of
training to the South, in a broader
sense? In connection with this, it is

well to bear in mind that slavery unconsciously taught the white man that
labour with the hands was something fit
for the Negro only, and something for
the white man to come into contact
with just as little as possible. It is true
that there was a large class of poor
white people who laboured with the
hands, but they did it because they
were not able to secure Negroes to
work for them; and these poor whites
were constantly trying to imitate the
slaveholding class in escaping labour,
as they, too, regarded it as anything
but elevating. But the Negro, in turn,
looked down upon the poor whites with
a certain contempt because they had to
work. The Negro, it is to be borne in
mind, worked under constant protest,
because he felt that his labour was being
unjustly requited; and he spent almost
as much effort in planning how to escape work as in learning how to work.
Labour with him was a badge of degra-

dation. The white man was held up
before him as the highest type of civilisation, but the Negro noted that this
highest type of civilisation himself did
little labour with the hand. Hence he
argued that, the less work he did, the
more nearly he would be like the white
man. Then, in addition to these influences, the slave system discouraged
labour-saving machinery. To use labour-
saving machinery, intelligence was required; and intelligence and slavery
were not on friendly terms. Hence the
Negro always associated labour with
toil, drudgery, something to be escaped.
When the Negro first became free, his
idea of education was that it was something that would soon put him in the
same position as regards work that his
recent master had occupied. Out of
these conditions grew the habit of putting off till to-morrow and the day after
the duty that should be done promptly
to-day. The leaky house was not re-

paired while the sun shone, for then the rain did not come through. While the rain was falling, no one cared to expose himself to stop the rain. The plough, on the same principle, was left where the last furrow was run, to rot and rust in the field during the winter. There was no need to repair the wooden chimney that was exposed to the fire, because water could be thrown on it when it was on fire. There was no need to trouble about the payment of a debt to-day, because it could be paid as well next week or next year. Besides these conditions, the whole South at the close of the war was without proper food, clothing, and shelter,— was in need of habits of thrift and economy and of something laid up for a rainy day.

To me it seemed perfectly plain that here was a condition of things that could not be met by the ordinary process of education. At Tuskegee we

became convinced that the thing to do
was to make a careful, systematic study
of the condition and needs of the
South, especially the Black Belt, and
to bend our efforts in the direction of
meeting these needs, whether we were
following a well-beaten track or were
hewing out a new path to meet conditions probably without a parallel in the
world. After eighteen years of experience and observation, what is the result? Gradually, but surely, we find
that all through the South the disposi-
tion to look upon labour as a disgrace
is on the wane; and the parents who
themselves sought to escape work are
so anxious to give their children training in intelligent labour that every
institution which gives training in
the handicrafts is crowded, and many
(among them Tuskegee) have to refuse
admission to hundreds of applicants.
The influence of Hampton and Tuskegee is shown again by the fact that

almost every little school at the remotest cross-road is anxious to be known as an industrial school, or, as some of the coloured people call it, an "industrous" school.

The social lines that were once sharply drawn between those who laboured with the hands and those who did not are disappearing. Those who formerly sought to escape labour, now when they see that brains and skill rob labour of the toil and drudgery once associated with it, instead of trying to avoid it, are willing to pay to be taught how to engage in it. The South is beginning to see labour raised up, dignified and beautified, and in this sees its salvation. In proportion as the love of labour grows, the large idle class, which has long been one of the curses of the South, disappears. As people become absorbed in their own affairs, they have less time to attend to everybody's else business.

The South is still an undeveloped and unsettled country, and for the next half-century and more the greater part of the energy of the masses will be needed to develop its material resources. Any force that brings the rank and file of the people to have a greater love of industry is therefore especially valuable. This result industrial education is surely bringing about. It stimulates production and increases trade,— trade between the races; and in this new and engrossing relation both forget the past. The white man respects the vote of a coloured man who does ten thousand dollars' worth of business; and, the more business the coloured man has, the more careful he is how he votes.

Immediately after the war there was a large class of Southern people who feared that the opening of the free schools to the freedmen and the poor whites — the education of the head alone — would result merely in increasing the class who sought to escape labour, and that the South would soon be overrun by the idle and vicious. But, as the results of industrial combined with academic training begin to show themselves in hundreds of communities that have been lifted up, these former prejudices against education are being removed. Many of those who a few years ago opposed Negro education are now among its warmest advocates.

This industrial training, emphasising, as it does, the idea of economic production, is gradually bringing the South to the point where it is feeding itself. After the war, what profit the South made out of the cotton crop it spent outside of the South to purchase food supplies,— meat, bread, canned vegetables, and the like,— but the improved methods of agriculture are fast changing this custom. With the newer methods of labour, which teach promptness and system and emphasise the worth of the beautiful, the moral value of the well-painted house, the fence with every paling and nail in its place, is bringing to bear upon the South an influence that is making it a new country in industry, education, and religion.

It seems to me I cannot do better than to close this chapter on the needs of the Southern Negro than by quoting from a talk given to the students at Tuskegee : —

" I want to be a little more specific in showing you what you have to do and how you must do it.

" One trouble with us is — and the same is true of any young people, no matter of what race or condition — we have too many stepping-stones. We step all the time, from one thing to another. You find a young man who is learning to make bricks ; and, if you ask him what he intends to do after learning the trade, in too many cases

95

he will answer, 'Oh, I am simply working at this trade as a stepping-stone to something higher.' You see a young man working at the brick-mason's trade, and he will be apt to say the same thing. And young women learning to be milliners and dressmakers will tell you the same. All are stepping to something higher. And so we always go on, stepping somewhere, never getting hold of anything thoroughly. Now we must stop this stepping business, having so many stepping-stones. Instead, we have got to take hold of these important industries, and stick to them until we master them thoroughly. There is no nation so thorough in their education as the Germans. Why? Simply because the German takes hold of a thing, and sticks to it until he masters it. Into it he puts brains and thought from morning to night. He reads all the best books and journals bearing on that particular study, and he

feels that nobody else knows so much
about it as he does.

"Take any of the industries I have
mentioned, that of brick-making, for example. Any one working at that trade
should determine to learn all there is to
be known about making bricks; read all
the papers and journals bearing upon
the trade; learn not only to make common hand-bricks, but pressed bricks,
fire-bricks,— in short, the finest and best
bricks there are to be made. And, when
you have learned all you can by reading
and talking with other people, you
should travel from one city to another,
and learn how the best bricks are made.
And then, when you go into business
for yourself, you will make a reputation
for being the best brick-maker in the
community; and in this way you will
put yourself on your feet, and become
a helpful and useful citizen. When a
young man does this, goes out into one
of these Southern cities and makes a

reputation for himself, that person wins a reputation that is going to give him a standing and position. And, when the children of that successful brick-maker come along, they will be able to take a higher position in life. The grandchildren will be able to take a still higher position. And it will be traced back to that grandfather who, by his great success as a brick-maker, laid a foundation that was of the right kind.

"What I have said about these two trades can be applied with equal force to the trades followed by women. Take the matter of millinery. There is no good reason why there should not be, in each principal city in the South, at least three or four competent coloured women in charge of millinery establishments. But what is the trouble?

"Instead of making the most of our opportunities in this industry, the temptation, in too many cases, is to be music-teachers, teachers of elocution, or something else that few of the race at present have any money to pay for, or the opportunity to earn money to pay for, simply because there is no foundation. But, when more coloured people succeed in the more fundamental occupations, they will then be able to make better provision for their children in what are termed the higher walks of life.

"And, now, what I have said about these important industries is especially true of the important industry of agriculture. We are living in a country where, if we are going to succeed at all, we are going to do so largely by what we raise out of the soil. The people in those backward countries I have told you about have failed to give attention to the cultivation of the soil, to the invention and use of improved agricultural implements and machinery. Without this no people can succeed. No race which fails to put brains into agriculture can succeed; and, if you want to realize the truth of this statement, go with me into the back districts of some of our Southern States, and you will find many people in poverty, and yet they are surrounded by a rich country.

" A race, like an individual, has got to have a reputation. Such a reputation goes a long way toward helping a race or an individual; and, when we have succeeded in getting such a reputation, we shall find that a great many of the discouraging features of our life will melt away.

" Reputation is what people think we are, and a great deal depends on that. When a race gets a reputation along certain lines, a great many things which now seem complex, difficult to attain, and are most discouraging, will disappear.

" When you say that an engine is a Corliss engine, people understand that that engine is a perfect piece of mechanical work,— perfect as far as human skill and ingenuity can make it perfect. You say a car is a Pullman car. That is all; but what does it mean? It means that the builder of that car got a reputation at the outset for thorough, perfect work, for turning out everything in first-class shape. And so with a race. You cannot keep back very long a race that has the reputation for doing perfect work in everything that it undertakes. And then we have got to get a reputation for economy. Nobody cares to associate with an individual in business or otherwise who has a reputation for being a trifling spendthrift, who spends his money for things that he can very easily get along without, who spends his money for clothing, gewgaws, superficialities, and other things, when he has not got the necessaries of life. We want to give the race a reputation for being frugal and saving in everything. Then we want to get a reputation for being industrious. Now, remember these three things: Get a reputation for being skilled. It will not do for a few here and there to have it: the race must have the reputation. Get a reputation for being so skilful, so industrious, that you will not leave a job until it is as nearly perfect as any one can make it. And then we want to make a reputation for the race for being honest, — honest at all times and under all circumstances. A few individuals here and there have it, a few communities have it; but the race as a mass must get it.

"You recall that story of Abraham Lincoln, how, when he was postmaster at a small village, he had left on his hands $1.50 which the government did not call for. Carefully wrapping up this money in a handkerchief, he kept it for ten years. Finally, one day, the government agent called for this amount; and it was promptly handed over to him by

Abraham Lincoln, who told him that during all those ten years he had never touched a cent of that money. He made it a principle of his life never to use other people's money. That trait of his character helped him along to the Presidency. The race wants to get a reputation for being strictly honest in all its dealings and transactions,— honest in handling money, honest in all its dealings with its fellow-men.

"And then we want to get a reputation for being thoughtful. This I want to emphasise more than anything else. We want to get a reputation for doing things without being told to do them every time. If you have work to do, think about it so constantly, investigate and read about it so thoroughly, that you will always be finding ways and means of improving that work. The average person going to work becomes a regular machine, never giving the matter of improving the methods of his work a thought. He is never at his work before the appointed time, and is sure to stop the minute the hour is up. The world is looking for the person who is thoughtful, who will say at the close of work hours: 'Is there not something else I can do for you? Can I not stay a little later, and help you?'

"Moreover, it is with a race as it is with an individual: it must respect itself if it would win the respect of others. There must be a certain amount of unity about a race, there must be a great amount of pride about a race, there must be a great deal of faith on the part of a race in itself. An individual cannot succeed unless he has about him a certain amount of pride,— enough pride to make him aspire to the highest and best things in life. An individual cannot succeed unless that individual has a great amount of faith in himself.

"A person who goes at an undertaking with the feeling that he cannot succeed is likely to fail. On the other hand, the individual who goes at an undertaking, feeling that he can succeed, is the individual who in nine cases out of ten does succeed. But, whenever you find an individual that is ashamed of his race, trying to get away from his race, apologising for being a member of his· race, then you find a weak individual. Where you find a race that is ashamed of itself, that is apologising for itself, there you will find a weak, vacillating race. Let us no longer have to apologise for our race in these or other matters. Let us think seriously and work seriously: then, as a race, we shall be thought of seriously, and, therefore, seriously respected."

CHAPTER V.

In this chapter I wish to show how, at Tuskegee, we are trying to work out the plan of industrial training, and trust I shall be pardoned the seeming egotism if I preface the sketch with a few words, by way of example, as to the expansion of my own life and how I came to undertake the work at Tuskegee.

My earliest recollection is of a small one-room log hut on a slave plantation in Virginia. After the close of the war, while working in the coal mines of West Virginia for the support of my mother, I heard, in some accidental way, of the Hampton Institute. When I learned that it was an institution where a black boy could study, could have a chance to work for his board, and at the same time be taught how to work and to realise the dignity of labor, I resolved to go there. Bidding my mother good-by, I started out one morning to find my way to Hampton, although I was almost penniless and had no definite idea as to where Hampton was. By walking, begging rides, and paying for a portion of the journey on the steam-cars, I finally succeeded in reaching the city of Richmond, Virginia. I was without money or friends. I slept on a sidewalk; and by working on a vessel the next day I earned money enough to continue my way to the institute, where I arrived with a capital of fifty cents. At Hampton I found the opportunity — in the way of buildings, teachers, and industries provided by the generous — to get training in the class-room and by practical touch with industrial life,— to learn thrift, economy, and push. I was surrounded by an atmosphere of business, Christian influence, and spirit of self-help, that seemed to have awakened every faculty in me, and caused me for the first time to realise what it meant to be a man instead of a piece of property.

While there, I resolved, when I had finished the course of training, I would go into the Far South, into the Black Belt of the South, and give my life to providing the same kind of opportunity for self-reliance, self-awakening, that I had found provided for me at Hampton.

My work began at Tuskegee, Alabama, in 1881, in a small shanty church, with one teacher and thirty students, without a dollar's worth of property. The spirit of work and of industrial thrift, with aid from the State and generosity from the North, have enabled us to develop an institution which now has about one thousand students, gathered from twenty-three States, and eighty-eight instructors. Counting students, instructors, and their families, we have a resident population upon the school grounds of about twelve hundred persons.

The institution owns two thousand three hundred acres of land, seven hundred of which are cultivated by student labor. There are six hundred head of live-stock, including horses, mules, cows, hogs, and sheep. There are over forty vehicles that have been made, and are now used, by the school. Training is given in twenty-six industries. There is work in wood, in iron, in leather, in tin; and all forms of domestic economy are engaged in. Students are taught mechanical and architectural drawing, receive training as agriculturists, dairymen, masons, carpenters, contractors, builders, as machinists, electricians, printers, dressmakers, and milliners, and in other directions.

The value of the property is $300,000. There are forty-two buildings, counting large and small, all of which, with the exception of four, have been erected by the labour of the students.

Since this work started, there has been collected and spent for its founding and support $800,000. The annual expense is now not far from $75,000. In a humble, simple manner the effort has been to place a great object-lesson in the heart of the South for the elevation of the coloured people, where there should be, in a high sense, that union of head, heart, and hand which has been the foundation of the greatness of all races since the world began.

What is the object of all this outlay? It must be first borne in mind that we have in the South a peculiar and unprecedented state of things. The cardinal needs among the eight million coloured people in the South, most of whom are to be found on the plantations, may be stated as food, clothing, shelter, education, proper habits, and a settlement of race relations. These millions of coloured people of the South cannot be reached directly by any missionary agent; but they can be reached by sending out among them strong, selected young men and women, with the proper training of head, hand, and heart, who will live among them and show them how to lift themselves up.

The problem that the Tuskegee Institute keeps before itself constantly is how to prepare these leaders. From the outset, in connection with religious and academic training, it has emphasised industrial, or hand, training as a means of finding the way out of present conditions. First, we have found the industrial teaching useful in giving the student a chance to work out a portion of his expenses while in school. Second, the school furnishes labour that has an economic value and at the same time gives the student a chance to acquire knowledge and skill while performing the labour. Most of all, we find the industrial system valuable in teaching economy, thrift, and the dignity of labour and in giving moral backbone to students. The fact that a student goes into the world conscious of his power to build a house or a wagon or to make a set of harness gives him a certain confidence and moral independence that he would not possess without such training.

A more detailed example of our methods at Tuskegee may be of interest. For example, we cultivate by student labour seven hundred acres of land. The object is not only to cultivate the land in a way to make it pay our boarding department, but at the same time to teach the students, in addition to the practical work, something of the chemistry of the soil, the best methods of drainage, dairying, cultivation of fruit, the care of live-stock and tools, and scores of other lessons needed by people whose main dependence is on agriculture.

Friends some time ago provided means for the erection of a large new chapel at Tuskegee. Our students made the bricks for this chapel. A large part of the timber was sawed by the students at our saw-mill, the plans were drawn by our teacher of architectural and mechanical drawing, and students did the brick-masonry, the plastering, the painting, the carpentry work, the tinning, the slating, and made most of the furniture. Practically, the whole chapel was built and furnished by student labour. Now the school has this building for permanent use, and the students have a knowledge of the trades employed in its construction.

While the young men do the kinds of work I have mentioned, young women to a large extent make, mend, and laundry the clothing of the young men. They also receive instruction in dairying, horticulture, and other valuable industries.

One of the objections sometimes urged against industrial education for the Negro is that it aims merely to teach him to work on the same plan that he worked on when in slavery. This is far from being the object at Tuskegee. At the head of each of the twenty-six industrial divisions we have an intelligent and competent instructor, just as we have in our history classes, so that the student is taught not only practical brick-masonry, for example, but also the underlying principles of that industry, the mathematics and the mechanical and architectural drawing. Or he is taught how to become master of the forces of nature, so that, instead of cultivating corn in the old way, he can use a corn cultivator that lays off the furrows, drops the corn into them, and covers it; and in this way he can do more work than three men by the old process of corn planting, while at the same time much of the toil is eliminated and labour is dignified. In a word, the constant aim is to show the student how to put brains into every process of labour, how to bring his knowledge of mathematics and the sciences in farming, carpentry, forging, foundry work, how to dispense as soon as possible with the old form of *ante-bellum* labour. In the erection of the chapel referred to, instead of letting the money which was given to us go into outside hands, we made it accomplish three objects: first, it provided the chapel; second, it gave the students a chance to get a practical knowledge of the trades connected with the building; and, third, it enabled them to earn something toward the payment of their board while receiving academic and industrial training.

Having been fortified at Tuskegee by education of mind, skill of hand, Christian character, ideas of thrift, economy, and push, and a spirit of independence, the student is sent out to become a centre of influence and light in showing the masses of our people in the Black Belt of the South how to lift themselves up. Can this be done? I give but one or two examples. Ten years ago a young coloured man came to the institute from one of the large plantation districts. He studied in the class-room a portion of the time, and received practical and theoretical training on the farm the remainder of the time. Having finished his course at Tuskegee, he returned to his plantation home, which was in a county where the coloured people outnumbered the whites six to one, as is true of many of the counties in the Black Belt of the South. He found the Negroes in debt. Ever since the war they had been mortgaging their crops for the food on which to live while the crops were growing. The majority of them were living from hand-to-mouth on rented land, in small one-room log cabins, and attempting to pay a rate of interest on their advances that ranged from fifteen to forty per cent. per annum. The school had been taught in

a wreck of a log cabin, with no apparatus, and had never been in session
longer than three months out of twelve.
He found the people, as many as eight
or ten persons, of all ages and conditions and of both sexes, huddled together and living in one-room cabins
year after year, and with a minister
whose only aim was to work upon the
emotions. One can imagine something
of the moral and religious state of the
community.

But the remedy! In spite of the evil
the Negro got the habit of work from
slavery. The rank and file of the race,
especially those on the Southern plantations, work hard; but the trouble is that
what they earn gets away from them in
high rents, crop mortgages, whiskey,
snuff, cheap jewelry, and the like. The
young man just referred to had been
trained at Tuskegee, as most of our
graduates are, to meet just this condition of things. He took the three

months' public school as a nucleus for his work. Then he organized the older people into a club, or conference, that held meetings every week. In these meetings he taught the people, in a plain, simple manner, how to save their money, how to farm in a better way, how to sacrifice,— to live on bread and potatoes, if necessary, till they could get out of debt, and begin the buying of lands.

Soon a large proportion of the people were in a condition to make contracts for the buying of homes (land is very cheap in the South) and to live without mortgaging their crops. Not only this; under the guidance and leadership of this teacher, the first year that he was among them they learned how and built, by contributions in money and labour, a neat, comfortable school-house that replaced the wreck of a log cabin formerly used. The following year the weekly meetings were continued, and

two months were added to the original
three months of school. The next year
two more months were added. The
improvement has gone on until these
people have every year an eight months'
school.

I wish my readers could have the
chance that I have had of going into
this community. I wish they could
look into the faces of the people, and
see them beaming with hope and de-
light. I wish they could see the two or
three room cottages that have taken the
place of the usual one-room cabin, see
the well-cultivated farms and the religious life of the people that now means
something more than the name. The
teacher has a good cottage and well-
kept farm that serve as models. In a
word, a complete revolution has been
wrought in the industrial, educational,
and religious life of this whole community by reason of the fact that they
have had this leader, this guide and

object-lesson, to show them how to take the money and effort that had hitherto been scattered to the wind in mortgages and high rents, in whiskey and gewgaws, and how to concentrate it in the direction of their own uplifting. One community on its feet presents an object-lesson for the adjoining communities, and soon improvements show themselves in other places.

Another student, who received academic and industrial training at Tuskegee, established himself, three years ago, as a blacksmith and wheelwright in a community; and, in addition to the influence of his successful business enterprise, he is fast making the same kind of changes in the life of the people about him that I have just recounted. It would be easy for me to fill many pages describing the influence of the Tuskegee graduates in every part of the South. We keep it constantly in the minds of our students and graduates that the industrial or material condition of the masses of our people must be improved, as well as the intellectual, before there can be any permanent change in their moral and religious life. We find it a pretty hard thing to make a good Christian of a hungry man. No matter how much our people "get happy" and "shout" in church, if they go home at night from church hungry, they are tempted to find something to eat before morning. This is a principle of human nature, and is not confined alone to the Negro. The Negro has within him immense power for self-up-lifting, but for years it will be necessary to guide him and stimulate his energies.

The recognition of this power led us to organise, five years ago, what is known as the Tuskegee Negro Conference,— a gathering that meets every February, and is composed of about eight hundred representatives, coloured men and women, from all sections of the Black

Belt. They come in ox-carts, mule-carts, buggies, on muleback and horse-back, on foot, by railroad. Some travel all night in order to be present. The matters considered at the conference are those that the coloured people have it in their own power to control,— such as the evils of the mortgage system, the one-room cabin, buying on credit, the importance of owning a home and of putting money in the bank, how to build school-houses and prolong the school term, and to improve their moral and religious condition. As a single example of the results, one delegate reported that since the conference was started, seven years ago, eleven people in his neighbourhood had bought homes, fourteen had gotten out of debt, and a number had stopped mortgaging their crops. Moreover, a school-house had been built by the people themselves, and the school term had been extended from three to six months; and, with a look of triumph, he exclaimed, "We's done libin' in de ashes."

Besides this Negro Conference for the masses of the people, we now have a gathering at the same time known as the Tuskegee Workers' Conference, composed of the officers and instructors of the leading coloured schools in the South. After listening to the story of the conditions and needs from the people themselves, the Workers' Conference finds much food for thought and discussion. Let me repeat, from its beginning, this institution has kept in mind the giving of thorough mental and religious training, along with such industrial training as would enable the student to appreciate the dignity of labour and become self-supporting and valuable as a producing factor, keeping in mind the occupations open in the South to the average man of the race.

This institution has now reached the point where it can begin to judge of the

value of its work as seen in its graduates. Some years ago we noted the
fact, for example, that there was quite a
movement in many parts of the South to
organise and start dairies. Soon after
this, we opened a dairy school where
a number of young men could receive
training in the best and most scientific
methods of dairying. At present we
have calls, mainly from Southern white
men, for twice as many dairymen as we
are able to supply. The reports indicate that our young men are giving the
highest satisfaction, and are fast changing and improving the dairy product in
the communities where they labour. I
have used the dairy industry simply as
an example. What I have said of this
industry is true in a larger or less degree of the others.

I cannot but believe, and my daily
observation and experience confirm me
in it, that, as we continue placing men
and women of intelligence, religion,

modesty, conscience, and skill in every community in the South, who will prove by actual results their value to the community, this will constitute the solution for many of the present political and sociological difficulties. It is with this larger and more comprehensive view of improving present conditions and laying the foundation wisely that the Tuskegee Normal and Industrial Institute is training men and women as teachers and industrial leaders.

Over four hundred students have finished the course of training at this institution, and are now scattered throughout the South, doing good work. A recent investigation shows that about 3,000 students who have taken only a partial course are doing commendable work. One young man, who was able to remain in school but two years, has been teaching in one community for ten years. During this time he has built a new school-house, extended the school term from three to seven months, and has bought a nice farm upon which he has erected a neat cottage. The example of this young man has inspired many of the coloured people in this community to follow his example in some degree; and this is one of many such examples.

Wherever our graduates and ex-students go, they teach by precept and example the necessary lesson of thrift, economy, and property-getting, and friendship between the races.

CHAPTER VI.

It has become apparent that the effort to put the rank and file of the coloured people into a position to exercise the right of franchise has not been the success that was expected in those portions of our country where the Negro is found in large numbers. Either the Negro was not prepared for any such wholesale exercise of the ballot as our recent amendments to the Constitution contemplated or the American people were not prepared to assist and encourage him to use the ballot. In either case the result has been the same.

On an important occasion in the life of the Master, when it fell to him to pronounce judgment on two courses of action, these memorable words fell from his lips: "And Mary hath chosen the better part." This was the supreme test in the case of an individual. It is the highest test in the case of a race or a nation.   Let us apply this test to the American Negro.

In the life of our Republic, when he has had the opportunity to choose, has it been the better or worse part? When in the childhood of this nation the Negro was asked to submit to slavery or choose death and extinction, as did the aborigines, he chose the better part, that which perpetuated the race.

When, in 1776, the Negro was asked to decide between British oppression and American independence, we find him choosing the better part; and Crispus Attucks, a Negro, was the first to shed his blood on State Street, Boston, that the white American might enjoy liberty forever, though his race remained in slavery. When, in 1814, at New Orleans, the test of patriotism came again, we find the Negro choosing the better part, General Andrew Jackson himself testifying that no heart was more loyal and no arm was more strong and useful in defence of righteousness.

When the long and memorable struggle came between union and separation, when he knew that victory meant freedom, and defeat his continued enslavement, although enlisting by the thousands, as opportunity presented itself, to fight in honourable combat for the cause of the Union and liberty, yet, when the suggestion and the temptation came to burn the home and massacre wife and children during the absence of the master in battle, and thus insure his liberty, we find him choosing the better part, and for four long years protecting and supporting the helpless, defenceless ones intrusted to his care.

When, during our war with Spain, the safety and honour of the Republic were threatened by a foreign foe, when the wail and anguish of the oppressed from a distant isle reached our ears, we find the Negro forgetting his own wrongs, forgetting the laws and customs that discriminate against him in his own country, and again choosing the better part. And, if any one would know how he acquitted himself in the field at Santiago, let him apply for answer to Shafter and Roosevelt and Wheeler. Let them tell how the Negro faced death and laid down his life in defence of honour and humanity. When the full story of the heroic conduct of the Negro in the Spanish-American War has been heard from the lips of Northern soldier and Southern soldier, from ex-abolitionist and ex-master, then shall the country decide whether a race that is thus willing to die for its country should not be given the highest opportunity to live for its country.

In the midst of all the complaints of suffering in the camp and field during the Spanish-American War, suffering from fever and hunger, where is the official or citizen that has heard a word of complaint from the lips of a black soldier? The only request that came from the Negro soldier was that he might be permitted to replace the white soldier when heat and malaria began to decimate the ranks of the white regiments, and to occupy at the same time the post of greater danger.

But, when all this is said, it remains true that the efforts on the part of his friends and the part of himself to share actively in the control of State and local government in America have not been a success in all sections. What are the causes of this partial failure, and what lessons has it taught that we may use in regard to the future treatment of the Negro in America?

In my mind there is no doubt but that we made a mistake at the beginning of our freedom of putting the emphasis on the wrong end. Politics and the holding of office were too largely emphasised, almost to the exclusion of every other interest.

I believe the past and present teach but one lesson,— to the Negro's friends and to the Negro himself,— that there is but one way out, that there is but one hope of solution; and that is for the Negro in every part of America to resolve from henceforth that he will throw aside every non-essential and cling only to essential,— that his pillar of fire by night and pillar of cloud by day shall be property, economy, education, and Christian character. To us just now these are the wheat, all else the chaff. The individual or race that owns the property, pays the taxes, possesses the intelligence and substantial character, is the one which is going to exercise the greatest control in government, whether he lives in the North or whether he lives in the South.

I have often been asked the cause of and the cure for the riots that have taken place recently in North Carolina and South Carolina.* I am not at all sure that what I shall say will answer these questions in a satisfactory way, nor shall I attempt to narrow my expressions to a mere recital of what has taken place in these two States. I prefer to discuss the problem in a broader manner.

In the first place, in politics I am a Republican, but have always refrained from activity in party politics, and expect to pursue this policy in the future. So in this connection I shall refrain, as I always have done, from entering upon any discussion of mere party politics. What I shall say of politics will bear upon the race problem and the civilisation of the South in the larger sense. In no case would I permit my political relations to stand in the way of my speaking and acting in the manner that I believe would be for the permanent interest of my race and the whole South.

In 1873 the Negro in the South had reached the point of greatest activity and influence in public life, so far as the mere holding of elective office was concerned. From that date those who have kept up with the history of the South have noticed that the Negro has steadily lost in the number of elective offices held. In saying this, I do not mean that the Negro has gone backward in the real and more fundamental things of life. On the contrary, he has gone forward faster than has been true of any other race in history, under anything like similar circumstances.

If we can answer the question as to why the Negro has lost ground in the matter of holding elective office in the South, perhaps we shall find that our reply will prove to be our answer also as to the cause of the recent riots in North Carolina and South Carolina.

The Future of the American Negro

Before beginning a discussion of the question I have asked, I wish to say that this change in the political influence of the Negro has continued from year to year, notwithstanding the fact that for a long time he was protected, politically, by force of federal arms and the most rigid federal laws, and still more effectively, perhaps, by the voice and influence in the halls of legislation of such advocates of the rights of the Negro race as Thaddeus Stevens, Charles Sumner, Benjamin F. Butler, James M. Ashley, Oliver P. Morton, Carl Schurz, and Roscoe Conkling, and on the stump and through the public press by those great and powerful Negroes, Frederick Douglass, John M. Langston, Blanche K. Bruce, John R. Lynch, P. B. S. Pinchback, Robert Browne Elliot, T. Thomas Fortune, and many others; but the Negro has continued for twenty years to have fewer representatives in the State and na-

tional legislatures. The reduction has
continued until now it is at the point
where, with few exceptions, he is without representatives in the law-making
bodies of the State and of the nation.

Now let us find, if we can, a cause
for this. The Negro is fond of saying
that his present condition is due to the
fact that the State and federal courts
have not sustained the laws passed for
the protection of the rights of his people; but I think we shall have to go
deeper than this, because I believe that
all agree that court decisions, as a rule,
represent the public opinion of the community or nation creating and sustain-
ing the court.

At the beginning of his freedom it
was unfortunate that those of the white
race who won the political confidence
of the Negro were not, with few exceptions, men of such high character as
would lead them to assist him in laying a firm foundation for his develop-

ment. Their main purpose appears to have been, for selfish ends in too many instances, merely to control his vote. The history of the reconstruction era will show that this was unfortunate for all the parties in interest.

It would have been better, from any point of view, if the native Southern white man had taken the Negro, at the beginning of his freedom, into his political confidence, and exercised an influence and control over him before his political affections were alienated.

The average Southern white man has an idea to-day that, if the Negro were permitted to get any political power, all the mistakes of the reconstruction period would be repeated. He forgets or ignores the fact that thirty years of acquiring education and property and character have produced a higher type of black man than existed thirty years ago.

But, to be more specific, for all practical purposes, there are two political parties in the South,—a black man's party and a white man's party. In saying this, I do not mean that all white men are Democrats; for there are some white men in the South of the highest character who are Republicans, and there are a few Negroes in the South of the highest character who are Democrats. It is the general understanding that all white men are Democrats or the equivalent, and that all black men are Republicans. So long as the colour line is the dividing line in politics, so long will there be trouble.

The white man feels that he owns most of the property, furnishes the Negro most of his employment, thinks he pays most of the taxes, and has had years of experience in government. There is no mistaking the fact that the feeling which has heretofore governed the Negro —that, to be manly and stand by his race, he must oppose the Southern white man with his vote — has had much to do with intensifying the opposition of the Southern white man to him.

The Southern white man says that it is unreasonable for the Negro to come to him, in a large measure, for his clothes, board, shelter, and education, and for his politics to go to men a thousand miles away. He very properly argues that, when the Negro votes, he should try to consult the interests of his employer, just as the Pennsylvania employee tries to vote for the interests of his employer. Further, that much of the education which has been given the Negro has been defective, in not preparing him to love labour and to earn his living at some special industry, and has, in too many cases, resulted in tempting him to live by his wits as a political creature or by trusting to his "influence" as a political time-server.

Then, there is no mistaking the fact, that much opposition to the Negro in politics is due to the circumstance that the Southern white man has not become accustomed to seeing the Negro exercise political power either as a voter or as an office-holder. Again, we want to bear it in mind that the South has not yet reached the point where there is that strict regard for the enforcement of the law against either black or white men that there is in many of our Northern and Western States. This laxity in the enforcement of the laws in general, and especially of criminal laws, makes such outbreaks as those in North Carolina and South Carolina of easy occurrence.

Then there is one other consideration which must not be overlooked. It is the common opinion of almost every black man and almost every white man that nearly everybody who has had anything to do with the making of laws bearing upon the protection of the Negro's vote has proceeded on the theory that all the black men for all time will vote the Republican ticket and that all the white men in the South will vote the Democratic ticket. In a word, all seem to have taken it for granted that the two races are always going to oppose each other in their voting.

In all the foregoing statements I have not attempted to define my own views or position, but simply to describe conditions as I have observed them, that might throw light upon the cause of our political troubles. As to my own position, I do not favour the Negro's giving up anything which is fundamental and which has been guaranteed to him by the Constitution of the United States. It is not best for him to relinquish any of his rights; nor would his doing so be best for the Southern white man. Every law placed in the Constitution of the United States was placed there to encourage and stimulate the highest citizenship. If the Negro is not stimulated and encouraged by just State and national laws to become the highest type of citizen, the result will be worse for the Southern white man than for the Negro. Take the State of South Carolina, for example, where nearly two-thirds of the population are Negroes. Unless these Negroes are encouraged by just election laws to become tax-payers and intelligent producers, the white people of South Carolina will have an eternal millstone about their necks.

In an open letter to the State Constitutional Convention of Louisiana, I wrote: "I am no politician. On the other hand, I have always advised my race to give attention to acquiring property, intelligence, and character, as the necessary bases of good citizenship, rather than to mere political agitation.

But the question upon which I write is out of the region of ordinary politics. It affects the civilisation of two races, not for to-day alone, but for a very long time to come.

"Since the war, no State has had such an opportunity to settle, for all time, the race question, so far as it concerns politics, as is now given to Louisiana. Will your convention set an example to the world in this respect? Will Louisiana take such high and just grounds in respect to the Negro that no one can doubt that the South is as good a friend to him as he possesses elsewhere? In all this, gentlemen of the convention, I am not pleading for the Negro alone, but for the morals, the higher life, of the white man as well.

"The Negro agrees with you that it is necessary to the salvation of the South that restrictions be put upon the ballot. I know that you have two serious problems before you; ignorant and corrupt

government, on the one hand; and, on
the other, a way to restrict the ballot
so that control will be in the hands of
the intelligent, without regard to race.
With the sincerest sympathy with you
in your efforts to find a good way out of
the difficulty, I want to suggest that no
State in the South can make a law that
will provide an opportunity or temptation for an ignorant white man to vote,
and withhold the opportunity or temptation from an ignorant coloured man,
without injuring both men. No State
can make a law that can thus be exe-
cuted without dwarfing, for all time, the
morals of the white man in the South.
Any law controlling the ballot that is not
absolutely just and fair to both races
will work more permanent injury to the
whites than to the blacks.

"The Negro does not object to an
educational and property test, but let
the law be so clear that no one clothed
with State authority will be tempted to

perjure and degrade himself by putting one interpretation upon it for the white man and another for the black man. Study the history of the South, and you will find that, where there has been the most dishonesty in the matter of voting, there you will find to-day the lowest moral condition of both races. First, there was the temptation to act wrongly with the Negro's ballot. From this it was an easy step to act dishonestly with the white man's ballot, to the carrying of concealed weapons, to the murder of a Negro, and then to the murder of a white man, and then to lynching. I entreat you not to pass a law that will prove an eternal millstone about the necks of your children. No man can have respect for the government and officers of the law when he knows, deep down in his heart, that the exercise of the franchise is tainted with fraud.

"The road that the South has been

compelled to travel during the last
thirty years has been strewn with thorns
and thistles. It has been as one grop-
ing through the long darkness into the
light. The time is not far distant when
the world will begin to appreciate the
real character of the burden that was
imposed upon the South in giving
the franchise to four millions of ignorant and impoverished ex-slaves. No
people was ever before given such a
problem to solve. History has blazed
no path through the wilderness that
could be followed. For thirty years we
have wandered in the wilderness. We
are now beginning to get out. But
there is only one road out; and all
makeshifts, expedients, profit and loss
calculations, but lead into swamps,
quicksands, quagmires, and jungles.
There is a highway that will lead both
races out into the pure, beautiful sunshine, where there will be nothing to
hide and nothing to explain, where both

races can grow strong and true and useful in every fibre of their being. I believe that your convention will find this highway, that it will enact a fundamental law that will be absolutely just and fair to white and black alike.

"I beg of you, further, that in the degree that you close the ballot-box against the ignorant you will open the school-house. More than one-half of the population of your State are Negroes. No State can long prosper when a large part of its citizenship is in ignorance and poverty, and has no interest in the government. I beg of you that you do not treat us as an alien people. We are not aliens. You know us. You know that we have cleared your forests, tilled your fields, nursed your children, and protected your families. There is an attachment between us that few understand. While I do not presume to be able to advise you, yet it is in my heart to say that, if your convention would do something that would prevent for all time strained relations between the two races, and would permanently settle the matter of political relations in one Southern State at least, let the very best educational opportunities be provided for both races; and add to this an election law that shall be incapable of unjust discrimination, at the same time providing that, in proportion as the ignorant secure education, property, and character, they will be given the right of citizenship. Any other course will take from one-half your citizens interest in the State, and hope and ambition to become intelligent producers and tax-payers, and useful and virtuous citizens. Any other course will tie the white citizens of Louisiana to a body of death.

" The Negroes are not unmindful of the fact that the poverty of the State prevents it from doing all that it desires for public education; yet I be-

lieve that you will agree with me that
ignorance is more costly to the State
than education, that it will cost Louisiana more not to educate the Negroes
than it will to educate them. In connection with a generous provision for
public schools, I believe that nothing
will so help my own people in your State
as provision at some institution for the
highest academic and normal training,
in connection with thorough training
in agriculture, mechanics, and domestic
economy. First-class training in agriculture, horticulture, dairying, stock-raising, the mechanical arts, and domestic
economy, would make us intelligent producers, and not only help us to contribute our honest share as tax-payers, but
would result in retaining much money
in the State that now goes outside for
that which can be as well produced at
home. An institution which will give
this training of the hand, along with
the highest mental culture, would soon

convince our people that their salvation is largely in the ownership of property and in industrial and business development, rather than in mere political agitation.

" The highest test of the civilisation of any race is in its willingness to extend a helping hand to the less fortunate. A race, like an individual, lifts itself up by lifting others up. Surely, no people ever had a greater chance to exhibit the highest Christian fortitude and magnanimity than is now presented to the people of Louisiana. It requires little wisdom or statesmanship to repress, to crush out, to retard the hopes and aspirations of a people; but the highest and most profound statesmanship is shown in guiding and stimulating a people, so that every fibre in the body and soul shall be made to contribute in the highest degree to the usefulness and ability of the State. It is along this line that I pray God the thoughts and activities of your convention may be guided."

As to such outbreaks as have recently occurred in North Carolina and South Carolina, the remedy will not be reached by the Southern white man merely depriving the Negro of his rights and privileges. This method is but superficial, irritating, and must, in the nature of things, be short-lived. The statesman, to cure an evil, resorts to enlightenment, to stimulation; the politician, to repression. I have just remarked that I favour the giving up of nothing that is guaranteed to us by the Constitution of the United States, or that is fundamental to our citizenship. While I hold to these views as strongly as any one, I differ with some as to the method of securing the permanent and peaceful enjoyment of all the privileges guaranteed to us by our fundamental law.

In finding a remedy, we must recog-

nise the world-wide fact that the Negro
must be led to see and feel that he must
make every effort possible, in every way
possible, to secure the friendship, the
confidence, the co-operation of his white
neighbour in the South. To do this, it
is not necessary for the Negro to become a truckler or a trimmer. The
Southern white man has no respect for
a Negro who does not act from principle. In some way the Southern white
man must be led to see that it is to his
interest to turn his attention more and
more to the making of laws that will, in
the truest sense, elevate the Negro. At
the present moment, in many cases,
when one attempts to get the Negro to
co-operate with the Southern white man,
he asks the question, "Can the people
who force me to ride in a Jim Crow car,
and pay first-class fare, be my best
friends?" In answering such questions, the Southern white man, as well
as the Negro, has a duty to perform.

In the exercise of his political rights I should advise the Negro to be temperate and modest, and more and more to do his own thinking.

I believe the permanent cure for our present evils will come through a property and educational test for voting that shall apply honestly and fairly to both races. This will cut off the large mass of ignorant voters of both races that is now proving so demoralising a factor in the politics of the Southern States.

But, most of all, it will come through industrial development of the Negro. Industrial education makes an intelligent producer of the Negro, who becomes of immediate value to the community rather than one who yields to the temptation to live merely by politics or other parasitical employments. It will make him soon become a property-holder; and, when a citizen becomes a holder of property, he becomes a conservative and thoughtful voter. He will more carefully consider the measures and individuals to be voted for. In proportion as he increases his property interests, he becomes important as a tax-payer.

There is little trouble between the Negro and the white man in matters of education; and, when it comes to his business development, the black man has implicit faith in the advice of the Southern white man. When he gets into trouble in the courts, which requires a bond to be given, in nine cases out of ten, he goes to a Southern white man for advice and assistance. Every one who has lived in the South knows that, in many of the church troubles among the coloured people, the ministers and other church officers apply to the nearest white minister for assistance and instruction. When by reason of mutual concession we reach the point where we shall consult the Southern white man about our politics as we now consult him about our business, legal and religious matters, there will be a change for the better in the situation.

The object-lesson of a thousand Negroes in every county in the South who own neat and comfortable homes, possessing skill, industry, and thrift, with money in the bank, and are large tax-payers co-operating with the white men in the South in every manly way for the development of their own communities and counties, will go a long way, in a few years, toward changing the present status of the Negro as a citizen, as well as the attitude of the whites toward the blacks.

As the Negro grows in industrial and business directions, he will divide in his politics on economic issues, just as the white man in other parts of the country now divides his vote. As the South grows in business prosperity it will divide its vote on economic issues, just as other sections of the country divide their vote. When we can enact laws that result in honestly cutting off the large ignorant and non-tax-paying vote, and when we can bring both races to the point where they will co-operate with each other in politics, as they do now in matters of business, religion, and education, the problem will be in a large measure solved, and political outbreaks will cease.

CHAPTER VII.

ONE of the great questions which Christian education must face in the South is the proper adjustment of the new relations of the two races. It is a question which must be faced calmly, quietly, dispassionately; and the time has now come to rise above party, above race, above colour, above sectionalism, into the region of duty of man to man, of American to American, of Christian to Christian.

I remember not long ago, when about five hundred coloured people sailed from the port of Savannah bound for Liberia, that the news was flashed all over the country, " The Negro has made up his mind to return to his own country," and that, "in this was the solution of the race problem in the South." But these short-sighted people forgot the fact that before breakfast that morning about five hundred more Negro children were born in the South alone.

And then, once in a while, somebody is so bold as to predict that the Negro will be absorbed by the white race. Let us look at this phase of the question for a moment. It is a fact that, if a person is known to have one per cent. of African blood in his veins, he ceases to be a white man. The ninety-nine per cent. of Caucasian blood does not weigh by the side of the one per cent. of African blood. The white blood counts for nothing. The person is a Negro every time. So it will be a very difficult task for the white man to absorb the Negro.

Somebody else conceived the idea of colonising the coloured people, of getting territory where nobody lived, putting the coloured people there, and letting them be a nation all by themselves. There are two objections to that. First, you would have to build one wall to keep the coloured people in, and another wall to keep the white people out. If you were to build ten walls around Africa to-day you could not keep the white people out, especially as long as there was a hope of finding gold there.

I have always had the highest respect for those of our race who, in trying to find a solution for our Southern problem, advised a return of the race to Africa, and because of my respect for those who have thus advised, especially Bishop Henry M. Turner, I have tried to make a careful and unbiassed study of the question, during a recent sojourn in Europe, to see what opportunities presented themselves in Africa for self-development and self-government.

I am free to say that I see no way out of the Negro's present condition in the South by returning to Africa. Aside from other insurmountable obstacles, there is no place in Africa for him to go where his condition would be improved. All Europe — especially England, France, and Germany — has been running a mad race for the last twenty years, to see which could gobble up the greater part of Africa; and there is practically nothing left. Old King Cetewayo put it pretty well when he said, " First come missionary, then come rum, then come traders, then come army "; and Cecil Rhodes has expressed the prevailing sentiment more recently in these words, " I would rather have land than 'niggers.' " And Cecil Rhodes is directly responsible for the killing of thousands of black natives in South Africa, that he might secure their land.

In a talk with Henry M. Stanley, the explorer, he told me that he knew no place in Africa where the Negroes of the United States might go to advantage; but I want to be more specific. Let us see how Africa has been divided, and then decide whether there is a

place left for us.   On the Mediterranean
coast of Africa, Morocco is an independent State, Algeria is a French possession, Tunis is a French protectorate,
Tripoli is a province of the Ottoman
Empire, Egypt is a province of Turkey.
On the Atlantic coast, Sahara is a
French protectorate, Adrar is claimed
by Spain, Senegambia is a French trad-
ing settlement, Gambia is a British
crown colony, Sierra Leone is a British
crown colony.   Liberia is a republic
of freed Negroes, Gold Coast and
Ashanti are British colonies and British
protectorates, Togoland is a German
protectorate, Dahomey is a kingdom
subject to French influence, Slave
Coast is a British colony and British
protectorate, Niger Coast is a British
protectorate, the Cameroons are trad-
ing settlements protected by Germany,
French Congo is a French protectorate,
Congo Free State is an international
African Association, Angola and Ben-

guela are Portuguese protectorates, and
the inland countries are controlled as
follows: The Niger States, Masina, etc.,
are under French protection; Land
Gandu is under British protection, administered by the Royal Haussan Niger
Company.

South Africa is controlled as follows:
Damara and Namaqua Land are German protectorates, Cape Colony is a
British colony, Basutoland is a Crown
colony, Bechuanaland is a British protectorate, Natal is a British colony,
Zululand is a British protectorate,
Orange Free State is independent, the
South African Republic is independent,
and the Zambesi is administered by the
British South African Company. Lou-
rence Marques is a Portuguese possession.

East Africa has also been disposed of
in the following manner: Mozambique
is a Portuguese possession, British Cen-
tral Africa is a British protectorate,

The Future of the American Negro

German East Africa is in the German
sphere of influence, Zanzibar is a sul-
tanate under British protection, British
East Africa is a British protectorate,
Somaliland is under British and Italian
protection, Abyssinia is independent.
East Soudan (including Nubia, Kordo-
fan, Darfur, and Wadai) is in the British sphere of influence. It will be
noted that, when one of these European
countries cannot get direct control over
any section of Africa, it at once gives
it out to the world that the country
wanted is in the "sphere of its influence," — a very convenient term. If
we are to go to Africa, and be under the
control of another government, I think
we should prefer to take our chances
in the "sphere of influence" of the
United States.

All this shows pretty conclusively
that a return to Africa for the Negro is
out of the question, even provided that
a majority of the Negroes wished to

go back, which they do not. The adjustment of the relations of the two races must take place here; and it is taking place slowly, but surely. As the Negro is educated to make homes and to respect himself, the white man will in turn respect him.

It has been urged that the Negro has inherent in him certain traits of character that will prevent his ever reaching the standard of civilisation set by the whites, and taking his place among them as an equal. It may be some time before the Negro race as a whole can stand comparison with the white in all respects,— it would be most remarkable, considering the past, if it were not so; but the idea that his objectionable traits and weaknesses are fundamental, I think, is a mistake. For, although there are elements of weakness about the Negro race, there are also many evidences of strength.

It is an encouraging sign, however,

when an individual grows to the point where he can hold himself up for personal analysis and study. It is equally encouraging for a race to be able to study itself,— to measure its weakness and strength. It is not helpful to a race to be continually praised and have its weakness overlooked, neither is it the most helpful thing to have its faults alone continually dwelt upon. What is needed is downright, straightforward honesty in both directions; and this is not always to be obtained.

There is little question that one of the Negroes' weak points is physical. Especially is this true regarding those who live in the large cities, North and South. But in almost every case this physical weakness can be traced to ignorant violation of the laws of health or to vicious habits. The Negro, who during slavery lived on the large plantations in the South, surrounded by restraints, at the close of the war came to the cities, and in many cases found the freedom and temptations of the city too much for him. The transition was too sudden.

When we consider what it meant to have four millions of people slaves to-day and freemen to-morrow, the wonder is that the race has not suffered more physically than it has. I do not believe that statistics can be so marshalled as to prove that the Negro as a race is physically or numerically on the decline. On the other hand, the Negro as a race is increasing in numbers by a larger percentage than is true of the French nation. While the death-rate is large in the cities, the birth-rate is also large; and it is to be borne in mind that eighty-five per cent. of these people in the Gulf States are in the country districts and smaller towns, and there the increase is along healthy and normal lines. As the Negro becomes educated, the high death-rate in the cities will disappear. For proof of this, I have only to mention that a few years ago no coloured man could get insurance in the large first-class insurance companies. Now there are few of these companies which do not seek the insurance of educated coloured men. In the North and South the physical intoxication that was the result of sudden freedom is giving way to an encouraging, sobering process; and, as this continues, the high death-rate will disappear even, in the large cities.

Another element of weakness which shows itself in the present stage of the civilisation of the Negro is his lack of ability to form a purpose and stick to it through a series of years, if need be,— years that involve discouragement as well as encouragement,— till the end shall be reached. Of course there are brilliant exceptions to this rule; but there is no question that here is an element of weakness, and the same, I think, would be true of any race with the Negro's history.

Few of the resolutions which are made in conventions, etc., are remembered and put into practice six months after the warmth and enthusiasm of the debating hall have disappeared. This, I know, is an element of the white man's weakness, but it is the Negro I am discussing, not the white man. Individually, the Negro is strong. Collectively, he is weak. This is not to be wondered at. The ability to succeed in organised bodies is one of the highest points in civilisation. There are scores of coloured men who can succeed in any line of business as individuals, or will discuss any subject in a most intelligent manner, yet who, when they attempt to act in an organised body, are utter failures.

But the weakness of the Negro which is most frequently held up to the public gaze is that of his moral character. No one who wants to be honest and at the same time benefit the race will deny that here is where the strengthening is to be done. It has become universally accepted that the family is the foundation, the bulwark, of any race. It should be remembered, sorrowfully withal, that it was the constant tendency of slavery to destroy the family life. All through two hundred and fifty years of slavery, one of the chief objects was to increase the number of slaves; and to this end almost all thought of morality was lost sight of, so that the Negro has had only about thirty years in which to develop a family life; while the Anglo-Saxon race, with which he is constantly being compared, has had thousands of years of training in home life. The Negro felt all through the years of bondage that he was being forcibly and unjustly deprived of the fruits of his labour. Hence he felt that anything he could get from the white man in return for this labour justly belonged to him. Since this was true, we must be patient in trying to teach him a different code of morals.

From the nature of things, all through slavery it was life in the future world that was emphasised in religious teaching rather than life in this world. In his religious meetings in *ante-bellum* days the Negro was prevented from discussing many points of practical religion which related to this world; and the white minister, who was his spiritual guide, found it more convenient to talk about heaven than earth, so very naturally that to-day in his religious meeting it is the Negro's feelings which are worked upon mostly, and it is description of the glories of heaven that occupy most of the time of his sermon.

Having touched upon some of the

weak points of the Negro, what are his strong characteristics? The Negro in America is different from most people for whom missionary effort is made, in that he works. He is not ashamed or afraid of work. When hard, constant work is required, ask any Southern white man, and he will tell you that in this the Negro has no superior. He is not given to strikes or to lockouts. He not only works himself, but he is unwilling to prevent other people from working.

Of the forty buildings of various kinds and sizes on the grounds of the Tuskegee Normal and Industrial Institute, in Alabama, as I have stated before, almost all of them are the results of the labour performed by the students while securing their academic education. One day the student is in his history class. The next day the same student, equally happy, with his trowel and in overalls, is working on a brick wall.

The Future of the American Negro

While at present the Negro may lack that tenacious mental grasp which enables one to pursue a scientific or mathematical investigation through a series of years, he has that delicate, mental feeling which enables him to succeed in oratory, music, etc.

While I have spoken of the Negro's moral weakness, I hope it will be kept in mind that in his original state his is an honest race. It was slavery that corrupted him in this respect. But in morals he also has his strong points.

Few have ever found the Negro guilty of betraying a trust. There are almost no instances in which the Negro betrayed either a Federal or a Confederate soldier who confided in him. There are few instances where the Negro has been entrusted with valuables when he has not been faithful. This country has never had a more loyal citizen. He has never proven himself a rebel. Should the Southern

States, which so long held him in slavery, be invaded by a foreign foe, the Negro would be among the first to come to the rescue.

Perhaps the most encouraging thing in connection with the lifting up of the Negro in this country is the fact that he knows that he is down and wants to get up, he knows that he is ignorant and wants to get light. He fills every school-house and every church which is opened for him. He is willing to follow leaders, when he is once convinced that the leaders have his best interest at heart.

Under the constant influence of the Christian education which began thirty-five years ago, his religion is every year becoming less emotional and more rational and practical, though I, for one, hope that he will always retain in a large degree the emotional element in religion.

During the two hundred and fifty

years that the Negro spent in slavery
he had little cause or incentive to accumulate money or property. Thirty-
five years ago this was something which
he had to begin to learn. While the
great bulk of the race is still without
money and property, yet the signs of
thrift are evident on every hand. Especially is this noticeable in the large
number of neat little homes which are
owned by these people on the outer
edges of the towns and cities in the
South.

I wish to give an example of the sort
of thing the Negro has to contend with,
however, in his efforts to lift himself up.

Not long ago a mother, a black
mother, who lived in one of our Northern States, had heard it whispered
around in her community for years
that the Negro was lazy, shiftless, and
would not work. So, when her only
boy grew to sufficient size, at consider-
able expense and great self-sacrifice,

she had her boy thoroughly taught the machinist's trade. A job was secured in a neighbouring shop. With dinner bucket in hand and spurred on by the prayers of the now happy-hearted mother, the boy entered the shop to begin his first day's work. What happened? Every one of the twenty white men threw down his tools, and deliberately walked out, swearing that he would not give a black man an opportunity to earn an honest living. Another shop was tried with the same result, and still another, the result ever the same. To-day this once promising, ambitious black man is a wreck,— a confirmed drunkard,— with no hope, no ambition. I ask, Who blasted the life of this young man? On whose hands does his life-blood rest? The present system of education, or rather want of education, is responsible.

Public schools and colleges should turn out men who will throw open the

doors of industry, so that all men, everywhere, regardless of colour, shall have
the same opportunity to earn a dollar
that they now have to spend it. I
know of a good many kinds of cow-
ardice and prejudice, but I know none
equal to this. I know not which is the
worst,— the slaveholder who perforce
compelled his slave to work without
compensation or the man who, by force
and strikes, compels his neighbour to
refrain from working for compensation.

The Negro will be on a different
footing in this country when it becomes
common to associate the possession of
wealth with a black skin. It is not
within the province of human nature
that the man who is intelligent and virtuous, and owns and cultivates the best
farm in his county, is the largest tax-
payer, shall very long be denied proper
respect and consideration. Those who
would help the Negro most effectually
during the next fifty years can do so

by assisting in his development along scientific and industrial lines in connection with the broadest mental and religious culture.

From the results of the war with Spain let us learn this, that God has been teaching the Spanish nation a terrible lesson. What is it? Simply this, that no nation can disregard the interest of any portion of its members without that nation becoming weak and corrupt. The penalty may be long delayed. God has been teaching Spain that for every one of her subjects that she has left in ignorance, poverty, and crime the price must be paid; and, if it has not been paid with the very heart of the nation, it must be paid with the proudest and bluest blood of her sons and with treasure that is beyond computation. From this spectacle I pray God that America will learn a lesson in respect to the ten million Negroes in this country.

The Future of the American Negro

The Negroes in the United States are, in most of the elements of civilisation, weak. Providence has placed them here not without a purpose. One object, in my opinion, is that the stronger race may imbibe a lesson from the weaker in patience, forbearance, and childlike yet supreme trust in the God of the Universe. This race has been placed here that the white man might have a great opportunity of lifting himself by lifting it up.

Out from the Negro colleges and industrial schools in the South there are going forth each year thousands of young men and women into dark and secluded corners, into lonely log schoolhouses, amidst poverty and ignorance; and though, when they go forth, no drums beat, no banners fly, no friends cheer, yet they are fighting the battles of this country just as truly and bravely as those who go forth to do battle against a foreign enemy.

If they are encouraged and properly supported in their work of educating the masses in the industries, in economy, and in morals, as well as mentally, they will, before many years, get the race upon such an intellectual, industrial, and financial footing that it will be able to enjoy without much trouble all the rights inherent in American citizenship.

Now, if we wish to bring the race to a point where it should be, where it will be strong, and grow and prosper, we have got to, in every way possible, encourage it. We can do this in no better way than by cultivating that amount of faith in the race which will make us patronise its own enterprises wherever those enterprises are worth patronising. I do not believe much in the advice that is often given that we should patronise the enterprises of our race without regard to the worth of those enterprises. I believe that the best way to bring the race to the point where it will compare with other races is to let it understand that, whenever it enters into any line of business, it will be patronised just in proportion as it makes that business as successful, as useful, as is true of any business enterprise conducted by any other race. The race that would grow strong and powerful must have the element of hero-worship in it that will, in the largest degree, make it honour its great men, the men who have succeeded in that race. I think we should be ashamed of the coloured man or woman who would not venerate the name of Frederick Douglass. No race that would not look upon such a man with honour and respect and pride could ever hope to enjoy the respect of any other race. I speak of this, not that I want my people to regard themselves in a narrow, bigoted sense, because there is nothing so hurtful to an individual or to a race as to get into the habit of feeling that there is no good except in its own race, but because I wish that it may have reasonable pride in all that is honourable in its history. Whenever you hear a coloured man say that he hates the people of the other race, there, in most instances, you will find a weak, narrow-minded coloured man. And, whenever you find a white man who expresses the same sentiment toward the people of other races, there, too, in almost every case, you will find a narrow-minded, prejudiced white man.

That person is the broadest, strongest, and most useful who sees something to love and admire in all races, no matter what their colour.

If the Negro race wishes to grow strong, it must learn to respect itself, not to be ashamed. It must learn that it will only grow in proportion as its members have confidence in it, in proportion as they believe that it is a coming race.

We have reached a period when educated Negroes should give more attention to the history of their race; should
devote more time to finding out the
true history of the race, and in collect-
ing in some museum the relics that
mark its progress. It is true of all
races of culture and refinement and
civilisation that they have gathered in
some place the relics which mark the
progress of their civilisation, which
show how they lived from period to
period. We should have so much pride
that we would spend more time in looking into the history of the race, more
effort and money in perpetuating in
some durable form its achievements, so
that from year to year, instead of looking back with regret, we can point to
our children the rough path through
which we grew strong and great.

We have a very bright and striking
example in the history of the Jews in
this and other countries. There is,

perhaps, no race that has suffered so much, not so much in America as in some of the countries in Europe. But these people have clung together. They have had a certain amount of unity, pride, and love of race; and, as the years go on, they will be more and more influential in this country,— a country where they were once despised, and looked upon with scorn and derision. It is largely because the Jewish race has had faith in itself. Unless the Negro learns more and more to imitate the Jew in these matters, to have faith in himself, he cannot expect to have any high degree of success.

I wish to speak upon another subject which largely concerns the welfare of both races, especially in the South,— lynching. It is an unpleasant subject; but I feel that I should be omitting some part of my duty to both races did I not say something on the subject.

For a number of years the South has

appealed to the North and to federal
authorities, through the public press,
from the public platform, and most
eloquently through the late Henry W.
Grady, to leave the whole matter of the
rights and protection of the Negro to
the South, declaring that it would see
to it that the Negro would be made
secure in his citizenship. During the
last half-dozen years the whole country,
from the President down, has been in-
clined more than ever to pursue this.
policy, leaving the whole matter of the
destiny of the Negro to the Negro
himself and to the Southern white
people, among whom the great bulk of
Negroes live.

By the present policy of non-inter-
ference on the part of the North and
the federal government the South is
given a sacred trust. How will she
execute this trust? The world is wait-
ing and watching to see. The question
must be answered largely by the pro-

tection it gives to the life of the Negro
and the provisions that are made for
his development in the organic laws of
the State. I fear that but few people
in the South realise to what an extent
the habit of lynching, or the taking of
life without due process of law, has
taken hold of us, and is hurting us, not
only in the eyes of the world, but in
our own moral and material growth.

Lynching was instituted some years
ago with the idea of punishing and
checking criminal assaults upon women.
Let us examine the facts, and see where
it has already led us and is likely further
to carry us, if we do not rid ourselves
of the evil. Many good people in the
South, and also out of the South, have
gotten the idea that lynching is re-
sorted to for one crime only. I have
the facts from an authoritative source.
During last year one hundred and
twenty-seven persons were lynched in
the United States. Of this number,

one hundred and eighteen were exe-
cuted in the South and nine in the
North and West. Of the total number
lynched, one hundred and two were
Negroes, twenty-three were whites, and
two Indians. Now, let every one interested in the South, his country, and the
cause of humanity, note this fact,—that
only twenty-four of the entire number
were charged in any way with the crime
of rape; that is, twenty-four out of one
hundred and twenty-seven cases of
lynching. Sixty-one of the remaining
cases were for murder, thirteen for
being suspected of murder, six for theft,
etc. During one week last spring, when
I kept a careful record, thirteen Negroes
were lynched in three of our Southern
States; and not one was even charged
with rape. All of these thirteen were
accused of murder or house-burning;
but in neither case were the men allowed to go before a court, so that their
innocence or guilt might be proven.

When we get to the point where four-fifths of the people lynched in our country in one year are for some crime other than rape, we can no longer plead and explain that we lynch for one crime alone.

Let us take another year, that of 1892, for example, when 241 persons were lynched in the whole United States. Of this number 36 were lynched in Northern and Western States, and 205 in our Southern States; 160 were Negroes, 5 of these being women. The facts show that, out of the 241 lynched, only 57 were even charged with rape or attempted rape, leaving in this year alone 184 persons who were lynched for other causes than that of rape.

If it were necessary, I could produce figures for other years. Within a period of six years about 900 persons have been lynched in our Southern States. This is but a few hundred short of the total number of soldiers who lost their lives in Cuba during the Spanish-American War. If we would realise still more fully how far this unfortunate evil is leading us on, note the classes of crime during a few months for which the local papers and the Associated Press say that lynching has been inflicted. They include "murder," "rioting," "incendiarism," "robbery," "larceny," "self-defence," "insulting women," "alleged stock-poisoning," "malpractice," "alleged barn - burning," "suspected robbery," "race prejudice," "attempted murder," "horse-stealing," "mistaken identity," etc.

The evil has so grown that we are now at the point where not only blacks are lynched in the South, but white men as well. Not only this, but within the last six years at least a half-dozen coloured women have been lynched. And there are a few cases where Negroes have lynched members of their

own race. What is to be the end of
all this? Furthermore, every lynching
drives hundreds of Negroes out of the
farming districts of the South, where
they make the best living and where
their services are of greatest value to
the country, into the already over-
crowded cities.

I know that some argue that the
crime of lynching Negroes is not confined to the South. This is true; and
no one can excuse such a crime as the
shooting of innocent black men in Illi-
nois, who were guilty of nothing, except
seeking labour. But my words just
now are to the South, where my home
is and a part of which I am. Let
other sections act as they will; I want
to see our beautiful Southland free from
this terrible evil of lynching. Lynching
does not stop crime. In the vicinity in
the South where a coloured man was
alleged recently to have committed the
most terrible crime ever charged against

a member of my race, but a few weeks previously five coloured men had been lynched for supposed incendiarism. If lynching was a cure for crime, surely the lynching of those five would have prevented another Negro from committing a most heinous crime a few weeks later.

We might as well face the facts bravely and wisely. Since the beginning of the world crime has been committed in all civilised and uncivilised countries, and a certain percentage of it will always be committed both in the North and in the South; but I believe that the crime of rape can be stopped. In proportion to the numbers and intelligence of the population of the South, there exists little more crime than in several other sections of the country; but, because of the lynching evil, we are constantly advertising ourselves to the world as a lawless people. We cannot disregard the teachings of the civilised world for eighteen hundred years, that the only way to punish crime is by law. When we leave this anchorage chaos begins.

I am not pleading for the Negro alone. Lynching injures, hardens, and blunts the moral sensibilities of the young and tender manhood of the South. Never shall I forget the remark by a little nine-year-old white boy, with blue eyes and flaxen hair. The little fellow said to his mother, after he had returned from a lynching: " I have seen a man hanged; now I wish I could see one burned." Rather than hear such a remark from one of my little boys, I would prefer to see him in his grave. This is not all. Every community guilty of lynching says in so many words to the governor, to the legislature, to the sheriff, to the jury, and to the judge: "We have no faith in you and no respect for you. We have no respect for the law which we helped to make."

In the South, at the present time, there is less excuse for not permitting the law to take its course where a Negro is to be tried than anywhere else in the world; for, almost without exception, the governors, the sheriffs, the judges, the juries, and the lawyers are all white men, and they can be trusted, as a rule, to do their duty. Otherwise, it is needless to tax the people to support these officers. If our present laws are not sufficient properly to punish crime, let the laws be changed; but that the punishment may be by lawfully constituted authorities is the plea I make. The history of the world proves that where the law is most strictly enforced there is the least crime: where people take the administration of the law into their own hands there is the most crime.

But there is still another side. The white man in the South has not only a serious duty and responsibility, but the Negro has a duty and responsibility in this matter. In speaking of my own people, I want to be equally frank; but I speak with the greatest kindness. There is too much crime among them. The figures for a given period show that in the United States thirty per cent. of the crime committed is by Negroes, while we constitute only about twelve per cent. of the entire population. This proportion holds good not only in the South, but also in Northern States and cities.

No race that is so largely ignorant and so recently out of slavery could, perhaps, show a better record, but we must face these plain facts. He is most kind to the Negro who tells him of his faults as well as of his virtues. A large percentage of the crime among us grows out of the idleness of our young men and women. It is for this reason that I have tried to insist upon some industry being taught in connection with their course of literary training. It is

vitally important now that every parent,
every teacher and minister of the gospel, should teach with unusual emphasis
morality and obedience to the law. At
the fireside, in the school-room, in the
Sunday-school, from the pulpit, and
in the Negro press, there should be
such a sentiment created regarding the
committing of crime against women
that no such crime could be charged
against any member of the race. Let it
be understood, for all time, that no one
guilty of rape can find sympathy or
shelter with us, and that none will be
more active than we in bringing to justice, through the proper authorities,
those guilty of crime. Let the criminal
and vicious element of the race have, at
all times, our most severe condemnation.
Let a strict line be drawn between the
virtuous and the criminal. I condemn,
with all the indignation of my soul, any
beast in human form guilty of assault-
ing a woman. I am sure I voice the

sentiment of the thoughtful of my race in this condemnation.

We should not, as a race, become discouraged. We are making progress. No race has ever gotten upon its feet without discouragements and struggles.

I should be a great hypocrite and a coward if I did not add that which my daily experience has taught me to be true ; namely, that the Negro has among many of the Southern whites as good friends as he has anywhere in the world. These friends have not forsaken us. They will not do so. Neither will our friends in the North. If we make ourselves intelligent, industrious, economical, and virtuous, of value to the community in which we live, we can and will work out our salvation right here in the South. In every community, by means of organised effort, we should seek, in a manly and honourable way, the confidence, the co-operation, the sympathy, of the best white people in the

South and in our respective communities. With the best white people and the best black people standing together, in favour of law and order and justice, I believe that the safety and happiness of both races will be made secure.

We are one in this country. The question of the highest citizenship and the complete education of all concerns nearly ten millions of my people and sixty millions of the white race. When one race is strong, the other is strong; when one is weak, the other is weak. There is no power that can separate our destiny. Unjust laws and customs which exist in many places injure the white man and inconvenience the Negro. No race can wrong another race, simply because it has the power to do so, without being permanently injured in its own morals. The Negro can endure the temporary inconvenience, but the injury to the white man is permanent. It is for the white man to save himself from this degradation that I plead. If a white man steals a Negro's ballot, it is the white man who is permanently injured. Physical death comes to the one Negro lynched in a county; but death of the morals — death of the soul — comes to those responsible for the lynching.

Those who fought and died on the battlefield for the freedom of the slaves performed their duty heroically and well, but a duty remains to those left. The mere fiat of law cannot make an ignorant voter an intelligent voter, cannot make a dependent man an independent man, cannot make one citizen respect another. These results will come to the Negro, as to all races, by beginning at the bottom and gradually working up to the highest possibilities of his nature.

In the economy of God there is but one standard by which an individual can succeed; there is but one for a race. This country expects that every race shall measure itself by the American standard. During the next half-century, and more, the Negro must continue passing through the severe American crucible. He is to be tested in his patience, his forbearance, his perseverance, his power to endure wrong, —to withstand temptations, to economise, to acquire and use skill,—his ability to compete, to succeed in commerce, to disregard the superficial for the real, the appearance for the substance, to be great and yet small, learned and yet simple, high and yet the servant of all. This,—this is the passport to all that is best in the life of our Republic; and the Negro must possess it or be barred out.

In working out his own destiny, while the main burden of activity must be with the Negro, he will need in the years to come, as he has needed in the past, the help, the encouragement, the guidance, that the strong can give the weak. Thus helped, those of both races in the South will soon throw off the shackles of racial and sectional prejudice, and rise above the clouds of ignorance, narrowness, and selfishness into that atmosphere, that pure sunshine, where it will be the highest ambition to serve man, our brother, regardless of race or previous condition.

CHAPTER VIII.

BEFORE ending this volume, I have deemed it wise and fitting to sum up in the following chapter all that I have attempted to say in the previous chapters, and to speak at the same time a little more definitely about the Negro's future and his relation to the white race.

All attempts to settle the question of the Negro in the South by his removal from this country have so far failed, and I think that they are likely to fail. The next census will probably show that we have about ten millions of Negroes in the United States. About eight millions of these are in the Southern States. We have almost a nation within a nation. The Negro population within the United States lacks but two millions of being as large as the whole population of Mexico. It is nearly twice as large as the population of the Dominion of Canada. It is equal to the combined population of Switzerland, Greece, Honduras, Nicaragua, Cuba, Uruguay, Santo Domingo, Paraguay, and Costa Rica. When we consider, in connection with these facts, that the race has doubled itself since its freedom, and is still increasing, it hardly seems possible for any one to consider seriously any scheme of emigration from America as a method of solution of our vexed race problem. At most, even if the government were to provide the means, but a few hundred thousand could be transported each year. The yearly increase in population would more than overbalance the number transplanted. Even if it did not, the time required to get rid of the Negro by this method would perhaps be fifty or seventy-five years. The idea is chimerical.

Some have advised that the Negro leave the South and take up his residence in the Northern States. I question whether this would leave him any better off than he is in the South, when all things are considered. It has been my privilege to study the condition of our people in nearly every part of America; and I say, without hesitation, that, with some exceptional cases, the Negro is at his best in the Southern States. While he enjoys certain privileges in the North that he does not have in the South, when it comes to the matter of securing property, enjoying business opportunities and employment, the South presents a far better opportunity than the North. Few coloured men from the South are as yet able to stand up against the severe and increasing competition that exists in the North, to say nothing of the unfriendly influence of labour organisations, which in some way prevents black men in the North, as a rule, from securing employment in skilled labour occupations.

Another point of great danger for the coloured man who goes North is in the matter of morals, owing to the numerous temptations by which he finds himself surrounded. He has more ways in which he can spend money than in the South, but fewer avenues of employment are open to him. The fact that at the North the Negro is confined to almost one line of employment often tends to discourage and demoralise the strongest who go from the South, and to make them an easy prey to temptation. A few years ago I made an examination into the condition of a settlement of Negroes who left the South and went to Kansas about twenty years ago, when there was a good deal of excitement in the South concerning emigration to the West. This settlement, I found, was much below the standard of that of a similar number of our people in the South. The only conclusion, therefore, it seems to me, which any one can reach, is that the Negroes, as a mass, are to remain in the Southern States. As a race, they do not want to

leave the South, and the Southern white
people do not want them to leave. We
must therefore find some basis of settlement that will be constitutional, just,
manly, that will be fair to both races in
the South and to the whole country.
This cannot be done in a day, a year, or
any short period of time. We can, it
seems to me, with the present light, decide upon a reasonably safe method
of solving the problem, and turn our
strength and effort in that direction.
In doing this, I would not have the
Negro deprived of any privilege guaranteed to him by the Constitution of the
United States. It is not best for the
Negro that he relinquish any of his
constitutional rights. It is not best for
the Southern white man that he should.

In order that we may, without loss of
time or effort, concentrate our forces in
a wise direction, I suggest what seems
to me and many others the wisest policy
to be pursued. I have reached these

conclusions by reason of my own obser-
vations and experience, after eighteen
years of direct contact with the leading
and influential coloured and white men
in most parts of our country. But I
wish first to mention some elements of
danger in the present situation, which
all who desire the permanent welfare of
both races in the South should carefully consider.

First.— There is danger that a certain class of impatient extremists among
the Negroes, who have little knowledge
of the actual conditions in the South,
may do the entire race injury by attempting to advise their brethren in the
South to resort to armed resistance or
the use of the torch, in order to secure
justice. All intelligent and well-consid-
ered discussion of any important question or condemnation of any wrong, both
in the North and the South, from the
public platform and through the press,
is to be commended and encouraged;

but ill-considered, incendiary utterances from black men in the North will tend to add to the burdens of our people in the South rather than relieve them.

Second. — Another danger in the South, which should be guarded against, is that the whole white South, including the wide, conservative, law-abiding element, may find itself represented before the bar of public opinion by the mob, or lawless element, which gives expression to its feelings and tendency in a manner that advertises the South throughout the world. Too often those who have no sympathy with such disregard of law are either silent or fail to speak in a sufficiently emphatic manner to offset, in any large degree, the unfortunate reputation which the lawless have too often made for many portions of the South.

Third.— No race or people ever got upon its feet without severe and constant struggle, often in the face of the

greatest discouragement. While passing through the present trying period
of its history, there is danger that a
large and valuable element of the Negro
race may become discouraged in the effort to better its condition. Every possible influence should be exerted to prevent this.

Fourth.— There is a possibility that
harm may be done to the South and to
the Negro by exaggerated newspaper
articles which are written near the scene
or in the midst of specially aggravating
occurrences. Often these reports are
written by newspaper men, who give the
impression that there is a race conflict
throughout the South, and that all Southern white people are opposed to the
Negro's progress, overlooking the fact
that, while in some sections there is
trouble, in most parts of the South there
is, nevertheless, a very large measure of
peace, good will, and mutual helpfulness.
In this same relation much can be done

to retard the progress of the Negro by a certain class of Southern white people, who, in the midst of excitement, speak or write in a manner that gives the impression that all Negroes are lawless, untrustworthy, and shiftless. As an example, a Southern writer said not long ago, in a communication to the New York *Independent*: "Even in small towns the husband cannot venture to leave his wife alone for an hour at night. At no time, in no place, is the white woman safe from insults and assaults of these creatures." These statements, I presume, represented the feelings and the conditions that existed at the time they were written in one community or county in the South. But thousands of Southern white men and women would be ready to testify that this is not the condition throughout the South, nor throughout any one State.

Fifth.— Under the next head I would mention that, owing to the lack of school opportunities for the Negro in the rural districts of the South, there is danger that ignorance and idleness may increase to the extent of giving the Negro race a reputation for crime, and that immorality may eat its way into the moral fibre of the race, so as to retard its progress for many years. In judging the Negro in this regard, we must not be too harsh. We must remember that it has only been within the last thirty-four years that the black father and mother have had the responsibility, and consequently the experience, of training their own children. That they have not reached perfection in one generation, with the obstacles that the parents have been compelled to overcome, is not to be wondered at.

Sixth.— As a final source of danger to be guarded against, I would mention my fear that some of the white people of the South may be led to feel that the way to settle the race problem is to repress the aspirations of the Negro by legislation of a kind that confers certain legal or political privileges upon an ignorant and poor white man and withholds the same privileges from a black man in the same condition. Such legislation injures and retards the progress of both races. It is an injustice to the poor white man, because it takes from him incentive to secure education and property as prerequisites for voting. He feels that, because he is a white man, regardless of his possessions, a way will be found for him to vote. I would label all such measures, "Laws to keep the poor white man in ignorance and poverty."

As the Talladega *News Reporter*, a Democratic newspaper of Alabama, recently said: "But it is a weak cry when the white man asks odds on intelligence over the Negro. When nature has already so handicapped the African in the race for knowledge, the cry of the

boasted Anglo-Saxon for still further
odds seems babyish. What wonder that
the world looks on in surprise, if not
disgust. It cannot help but say, if our
contention be true that the Negro is an
inferior race, that the odds ought to be
on the other side, if any are to be given.
And why not? No, the thing to do —
the only thing that will stand the test
of time — is to do right, exactly right,
let come what will. And that right
thing, as it seems to me, is to place
a fair educational qualification before
every citizen,— one that is self-testing,
and not dependent on the wishes of
weak men, letting all who pass the test
stand in the proud ranks of American
voters, whose votes shall be counted as
cast, and whose sovereign will shall be
maintained as law by all the powers
that be. Nothing short of this will
do. Every exemption, on whatsoever
ground, is an outrage that can only rob
some legitimate voter of his rights."

Such laws as have been made — as an example, in Mississippi — with the " understanding " clause hold out a temptation for the election officer to perjure and degrade himself by too often deciding that the ignorant white man does understand the Constitution when it is read to him and that the ignorant black man does not. By such a law the State not only commits a wrong against its black citizens; it injures the morals of its white citizens by conferring such a power upon any white man who may happen to be a judge of elections.

Such laws are hurtful, again, because they keep alive in the heart of the black man the feeling that the white man means to oppress him. The only safe way out is to set a high standard as a test of citizenship, and require blacks and whites alike to come up to it. When this is done, both will have a higher respect for the election laws and those who make them. I do not believe

that, with his centuries of advantage
over the Negro in the opportunity to
acquire property and education as prerequisites for voting, the average white
man in the South desires that any
special law be passed to give him advantage over the Negro, who has had
only a little more than thirty years in
which to prepare himself for citizenship.
In this relation another point of danger
is that the Negro has been made to feel
that it is his duty to oppose continually
the Southern white man in politics, even
in matters where no principle is involved,
and that he is only loyal to his own race
and acting in a manly way when he is
opposing him. Such a policy has proved
most hurtful to both races. Where it
is a matter of principle, where a question of right or wrong is involved, I
would advise the Negro to stand by
principle at all hazards. A Southern
white man has no respect for or confidence in a Negro who acts merely for

policy's sake; but there are many cases — and the number is growing — where the Negro has nothing to gain and much to lose by opposing the Southern white man in many matters that relate to government.

Under these six heads I believe I have stated some of the main points which all high-minded white men and black men, North and South, will agree need our most earnest and thoughtful consideration, if we would hasten, and not hinder, the progress of our country.

As to the policy that should be pursued in a larger sense,— on this subject I claim to possess no superior wisdom or unusual insight. I may be wrong; I may be in some degree right.

In the future, more than in the past, we want to impress upon the Negro the importance of identifying himself more closely with the interests of the South, — the importance of making himself part of the South and at home in it.

Heretofore, for reasons which were natural and for which no one is especially to blame, the coloured people have been too much like a foreign nation residing in the midst of another nation. If William Lloyd Garrison, Wendell Phillips, and George L. Stearns were alive to-day, I feel sure that each one of them would advise the Negroes to identify their interests as far as possible with those of the Southern white man, always with the understanding that this should be done where no question of right and wrong is involved. In no other way, it seems to me, can we get a foundation for peace and progress. He who advises against this policy will advise the Negro to do that which no people in history who have succeeded have done. The white man, North or South, who advises the Negro against it advises him to do that which he himself has not done. The bed-rock upon which every individual rests his chances

of success in life is securing the friendship, the confidence, the respect, of his
next-door neighbour of the little community in which he lives. Almost the
whole problem of the Negro in the
South rests itself upon the fact as to
whether the Negro can make himself of
such indispensable service to his neighbour and the community that no one can
fill his place better in the body politic.
There is at present no other safe course
for the black man to pursue. If the
Negro in the South has a friend in his
white neighbour and a still larger number of friends in his community, he has
a protection and a guarantee of his
rights that will be more potent and
more lasting than any our Federal Con-
gress or any outside power can confer.

In a recent editorial the London
Times, in discussing affairs in the Trans-
vaal, South Africa, where Englishmen
have been denied certain privileges by
the Boers, says: " England is too saga-

cious not to prefer a gradual reform from within, even should it be less rapid than most of us might wish, to the most sweeping redress of grievances imposed from without. Our object is to obtain fair play for the outlanders, but the best way to do it is to enable them to help themselves." This policy, I think, is equally safe when applied to conditions in the South. The foreigner who comes to America, as soon as possible, identifies himself in business, education, politics, and sympathy with the community in which he settles. As I have said, we have a conspicuous example of this in the case of the Jews. Also, the Negro in Cuba has practically settled the race question there, because he has made himself a part of Cuba in thought and action.

What I have tried to indicate cannot be accomplished by any sudden revolution of methods, but it does seem that the tendency more and more should be in this direction.   If a practical example is wanted in the direction that I favour, I will mention one. The North sends thousands of dollars into the South each year, for the education of the Negro. The teachers in most of the academic schools of the South are supported by the North, or Northern men and women of the highest Christian culture and most unselfish devotion. The Negro owes them a debt of gratitude which can never be paid. The various missionary societies in the North have done a work which, in a large degree, has been the salvation of the South; and the result will appear in future generations more than in this. We have now reached the point in the South where, I believe, great good could be accomplished by changing the attitude of the white people toward the Negro and of the Negro toward the whites, if a few white teachers of high character would take an active interest in the work of these high schools.   Can this be done? Yes. The medical school connected with Shaw University at Raleigh, North Carolina, has from the first had as instructors and professors, almost exclusively, Southern white doctors, who reside in Raleigh; and they have given the highest satisfaction. This gives the people of Raleigh the feeling that this is their school, and not something located in, but not a part of, the South. In Augusta, Georgia, the Payne Institute, one of the best colleges for our people, is officered and taught almost wholly by Southern white men and women. The Presbyterian Theological School at Tuscaloosa, Alabama, has all Southern white men as instructors. Some time ago, at the Calhoun School in Alabama, one of the leading white men in the county was given an important position in the school. Since then the feeling of the white people in the county has greatly changed toward the school.

We must admit the stern fact that at present the Negro, through no choice of his own, is living among another race which is far ahead of him in education, property, experience, and favourable condition; further, that the Negro's present condition makes him dependent upon the white people for most of the things necessary to sustain life, as well as for his common school education. In all history, those who have possessed the property and intelligence have exercised the greatest control in government, regardless of colour, race, or geographical location. This being the case, how can the black man in the South improve his present condition? And does the Southern white man want him to improve it?

The Negro in the South has it within his power, if he properly utilises the forces at hand, to make of himself such a valuable factor in the life of the South that he will not have to seek privileges,

they will be freely conferred upon him.
To bring this about, the Negro must
begin at the bottom and lay a sure
foundation, and not be lured by any
temptation into trying to rise on a false
foundation. While the Negro is laying
this foundation he will need help, sympathy, and simple justice. Progress by
any other method will be but temporary and superficial, and the latter end
of it will be worse than the beginning.
American slavery was a great curse
to both races, and I would be the last
to apologise for it; but, in the presence
of God, I believe that slavery laid the
foundation for the solution of the problem that is now before us in the South.
During slavery the Negro was taught
every trade, every industry, that constitutes the foundation for making a living.
Now, if on this foundation — laid in
rather a crude way, it is true, but a
foundation, nevertheless — we can gradually build and improve, the future for

us is bright. Let me be more specific.
Agriculture is, or has been, the basic
industry of nearly every race or nation
that has succeeded. The Negro got
a knowledge of this during slavery.
Hence, in a large measure, he is in
possession of this industry in the South
to-day. The Negro can buy land in
the South, as a rule, wherever the white
man can buy it, and at very low
prices. Now, since the bulk of our
people already have a foundation in agriculture, they are at their best when
living in the country, engaged in agricultural pursuits. Plainly, then, the best
thing, the logical thing, is to turn the
larger part of our strength in a direction that will make the Negro among
the most skilled agricultural people in
the world. The man who has learned
to do something better than any one
else, has learned to do a common thing
in an uncommon manner, is the man
who has a power and influence that no

adverse circumstances can take from him.
The Negro who can make himself so
conspicuous as a successful farmer, a
large tax-payer, a wise helper of his fellow-men, as to be placed in a position of
trust and honour, whether the position
be political or otherwise, by natural se-
lection, is a hundred-fold more secure in
that position than one placed there by
mere outside force or pressure. I know
a Negro, Hon. Isaiah T. Montgomery,
in Mississippi, who is mayor of a
town. It is true that this town, at
present, is composed almost wholly of
Negroes. Mr. Montgomery is mayor of
this town because his genius, thrift, and
foresight have created the town ; and he
is held and supported in his office by a
charter, granted by the State of Mississippi, and by the vote and public sentiment of the community in which he
lives.

Let us help the Negro by every
means possible to acquire such an edu-

cation in farming, dairying, stock-raising, horticulture, etc., as will enable him
to become a model in these respects
and place him near the top in these industries, and the race problem would
in a large part be settled, or at least
stripped of many of its most perplexing
elements. This policy would also tend
to keep the Negro in the country and
smaller towns, where he succeeds best,
and stop the influx into the large cities,
where he does not succeed so well.
The race, like the individual, that produces something of superior worth that
has a common human interest, makes a
permanent place for itself, and is bound
to be recognised.

At a county fair in the South not
long ago I saw a Negro awarded the
first prize by a jury of white men, over
white competitors, for the production
of the best specimen of Indian corn.
Every white man at this fair seemed to
be pleased and proud of the achieve-

ment of this Negro, because it was apparent that he had done something that would add to the wealth and comfort of the people of both races in that county. At the Tuskegee Normal and Industrial Institute in Alabama we have a department devoted to training men in the science of agriculture; but what we are doing is small when compared with what should be done at Tuskegee and at other educational centres. In a material sense the South is still an undeveloped country. While race prejudice is strongly exhibited in many directions, in the matter of business, of commercial and industrial development, there is very little obstacle in the Negro's way. A Negro who produces or has for sale something that the community wants finds customers among white people as well as black people. A Negro can borrow money at the bank with equal security as readily as a white man can. A bank in Birmingham,

The Future of the American Negro

Alabama, that has now existed ten years, is officered and controlled wholly by Negroes. This bank has white borrowers and white depositors. A graduate of the Tuskegee Institute keeps a well-appointed grocery store in Tuskegee, and he tells me that he sells about as many goods to the one race as to the other. What I have said of the opening that awaits the Negro in the direction of agriculture is almost equally true of mechanics, manufacturing, and all the domestic arts. The field is before him and right about him. Will he occupy it? Will he "cast down his bucket where he is"? Will his friends North and South encourage him and prepare him to occupy it? Every city in the South, for example, would give support to a first-class architect or house-builder or contractor of our race. The architect and contractor would not only receive support, but, through his example, numbers of young coloured men would learn such trades as carpentry, brick-masonry, plastering, painting, etc., and the race would be put into a position to hold on to many of the industries which it is now in danger of losing, because in too many cases brains, skill, and dignity are not imparted to the common occupations of life that are about his very door. Any individual or race that does not fit itself to occupy in the best manner the field or service that is right about it will sooner or later be asked to move on, and let some one else occupy it.

But it is asked, Would you confine the Negro to agriculture, mechanics, and domestic arts, etc.? Not at all; but along the lines that I have mentioned is where the stress should be laid just now and for many years to come. We will need and must have many teachers and ministers, some doctors and lawyers and statesmen; but these professional men will have a constituency or a foun-

dation from which to draw support just
in proportion as the race prospers along
the economic lines that I have mentioned. During the first fifty or one
hundred years of the life of any people
are not the economic occupations always given the greater attention? This
is not only the historic, but, I think, the
common-sense view. If this generation
will lay the material foundation, it will
be the quickest and surest way for the
succeeding generation to succeed in the
cultivation of the fine arts, and to surround itself even with some of the
luxuries of life, if desired. What the
race now most needs, in my opinion, is
a whole army of men and women well
trained to lead and at the same time
infuse themselves into agriculture, mechanics, domestic employment, and
business. As to the mental training
that these educated leaders should be
equipped with, I should say, Give them
all the mental training and culture that

the circumstances of individuals will allow,— the more, the better. No race can permanently succeed until its mind is awakened and strengthened by the ripest thought. But I would constantly have it kept in the thoughts of those who are educated in books that a large proportion of those who are educated should be so trained in hand that they can bring this mental strength and knowledge to bear upon the physical conditions in the South which I have tried to emphasise.

Frederick Douglass, of sainted memory, once, in addressing his race, used these words: " We are to prove that we can better our own condition. One way to do this is to accumulate property. This may sound to you like a new gospel. You have been accustomed to hear that money is the root of all evil, etc. On the other hand, property — money, if you please — will purchase for us the only condition by

which any people can rise to the dignity
of genuine manhood; for without property there can be no leisure, without
leisure there can be no thought, without
thought there can be no invention,
without invention there can be no
progress."

The Negro should be taught that
material development is not an end,
but simply a means to an end. As
Professor W. E. B. DuBois puts it,
" The idea should not be simply to make
men carpenters, but to make carpenters
men." The Negro has a highly religious temperament; but what he needs
more and more is to be convinced of
the importance of weaving his religion
and morality into the practical affairs
of daily life. Equally as much does he
need to be taught to put so much intelligence into his labour that he will see
dignity and beauty in the occupation,
and love it for its own sake. The Negro needs to be taught that more of the

religion that manifests itself in his happiness in the prayer-meeting should be made practical in the performance of his daily task. The man who owns a home and is in the possession of the elements by which he is sure of making a daily living has a great aid to a moral and religious life. What bearing will all this have upon the Negro's place in the South as a citizen and in the enjoyment of the privileges which our government confers?

To state in detail just what place the black man will occupy in the South as a citizen, when he has developed in the direction named, is beyond the wisdom of any one. Much will depend upon the sense of justice which can be kept alive in the breast of the American people. Almost as much will depend upon the good sense of the Negro himself. That question, I confess, does not give me the most concern just now. The important and pressing question is, Will the Negro with his own help and that of his friends take advantage of the opportunities that now surround him? When he has done this, I believe that, speaking of his future in general terms, he will be treated with justice, will be given the protection of the law, and will be given the recognition in a large measure which his usefulness and ability warrant. If, fifty years ago, any one had predicted that the Negro would have received the recognition and honour which individuals have already received, he would have been laughed at as an idle dreamer. Time, patience, and constant achievement are great factors in the rise of a race.

I do not believe that the world ever takes a race seriously, in its desire to enter into the control of the government of a nation in any large degree, until a large number of individuals, members of that race, have demonstrated, beyond question, their ability to control and develop individual business enterprises. When a number of Negroes rise to the point where they own and operate the most successful farms, are among the largest tax-payers in their county, are moral and intelligent, I do not believe that in many portions of the South such men need long be denied the right of saying by their votes how they prefer their property to be taxed and in choosing those who are to make and administer the laws.

In a certain town in the South, recently, I was on the street in company with the most prominent Negro in the town. While we were together, the mayor of the town sought out the black man, and said, " Next week we are going to vote on the question of issuing bonds to secure water-works for this town ; you must be sure to vote on the day of election." The mayor did not suggest whether he must vote " yes " or " no"; he knew from the very fact that this

Negro man owned nearly a block of the most valuable property in the town that he would cast a safe, wise vote on this important proposition. This white man knew that, because of this Negro's property interests in the city, he would cast his vote in the way he thought would benefit every white and black citizen in the town, and not be controlled by influences a thousand miles away. But a short time ago I read letters from nearly every prominent white man in Birmingham, Alabama, asking that the Rev. W. R. Pettiford, a Negro, be appointed to a certain important federal office. What is the explanation of this? Mr. Pettiford for nine years has been the president of the Negro bank in Birmingham to which I have alluded. During these nine years these white citizens have had the opportunity of seeing that Mr. Pettiford could manage successfully a private business, and that he had proven himself a conservative, thoughtful citi-

zen; and they were willing to trust
him in a public office. Such individual examples will have to be multiplied until they become the rule rather
than the exception. While we are mul-
tiplying these examples, the Negro must
keep a strong and courageous heart.
He cannot improve his condition by
any short-cut course or by artificial
methods. Above all, he must not be
deluded into the temptation of believ-
ing that his condition can be permanently improved by a mere battledore
and shuttlecock of words or by any
process of mere mental gymnastics or
oratory alone. What is desired, along
with a logical defence of his cause, are
deeds, results,— multiplied results,— in
the direction of building himself up, so
as to leave no doubt in the minds of any
one of his ability to succeed.

An important question often asked is,
Does the white man in the South want
the Negro to improve his present con-

dition? I say, "Yes." From the Montgomery (Alabama) *Daily Advertiser* I clip the following in reference to the closing of a coloured school in a town in Alabama:—

"EUFAULA, May 25, 1899.

"The closing exercises of the city coloured public school were held at St. Luke's A. M. E. Church last night, and were witnessed by a large gathering, including many white. The recitations by the pupils were excellent, and the music was also an interesting feature. Rev. R. T. Pollard delivered the address, which was quite an able one; and the certificates were presented by Professor T. L. McCoy, white, of the Sanford Street School. The success of the exercises reflects great credit on Professor S. M. Murphy, the principal, who enjoys a deservedly good reputation as a capable and efficient educator."

I quote this report, not because it is the exception, but because such marks of interest in the education of the Negro on the part of the Southern white people can be seen almost every day in the local papers. Why should white people, by their presence, words, and many other things, encourage the black man to get education, if they do not desire him to improve his condition?

The Payne Institute in Augusta, Georgia, an excellent institution, to which I have already referred, is supported almost wholly by the Southern white Methodist church. The Southern white Presbyterians support a theological school at Tuscaloosa, Alabama, for Negroes. For a number of years the Southern white Baptists have contributed toward Negro education. Other denominations have done the same. If these people do not want the Negro educated to a high standard, there is no reason why they should act the hypocrite in these matters.

As barbarous as some of the lynch-

ings in the South have been, Southern
white men here and there, as well as
newspapers, have spoken out strongly
against lynching. I quote from the
address of the Rev. Mr. Vance, of
Nashville, Tennessee, delivered before
the National Sunday School Union
in Atlanta, not long since, as an example : —

"And yet, as I stand here to-night,
a Southerner speaking for my section,
and addressing an audience from all
sections, there is one foul blot upon the
fair fame of the South, at the bare mention of which the heart turns sick and
the cheek is crimsoned with shame. I
want to lift my voice to-night in loud
and long and indignant protest against
the awful horror of mob violence, which
the other day reached the climax of its
madness and infamy in a deed as black
and brutal and barbarous as can be
found in the annals of human crime.

"I have a right to speak on the subject, and I propose to be heard. The time has come for every lover of the South to set the might of an angered and resolute manhood against the shame and peril of the lynch demon. These people, whose fiendish glee taunts their victim as his flesh crackles in the flames, do not represent the South. I have not a syllable of apology for the sickening crime they meant to avenge. But it is high time we were learning that lawlessness is no remedy for crime. For one, I dare to believe that the people of my section are able to cope with crime, however treacherous and defiant, through their courts of justice; and I plead for the masterful sway of a righteous and exalted public sentiment that shall class lynch law in the category with crime."

It is a notable and praiseworthy fact that no Negro educated in any of our larger institutions of learning in the South has been charged with any of the recent crimes connected with assaults upon females.

If we go on making progress in the directions that I have tried to indicate, more and more the South will be drawn to one course. As I have already said, it is not for the best interests of the white race of the South that the Negro be deprived of any privilege guaranteed him by the Constitution of the United States. This would put upon the South a burden under which no government could stand and prosper. Every article in our federal Constitution was placed there with a view of stimulating and encouraging the highest type of citizenship. To permanently tax the Negro without giving him the right to vote as fast as he qualifies himself in education and property for voting would work the alienation of the affections of the Negro from the States in which he lives, and would be the reversal of the fundamental principles of government for which our States have stood. In other ways than this the injury would be as great to the white man as to the Negro. Taxation without the hope of becoming a voter would take away from one-third the citizens of the Gulf States their interest in government and their stimulant to become taxpayers or to secure education, and thus be able and willing to bear their share of the cost of education and government, which now weighs so heavily upon the white tax-payers of the South. The more the Negro is stimulated and encouraged, the sooner will he be able to bear a larger share of the burdens of the South. We have recently had before us an example, in the case of Spain, of a government that left a large portion of its citizens in ignorance, and neglected their highest interests.

As I have said elsewhere, there is no escape through law of man or God from the inevitable:—

"The laws of changeless justice bind
Oppressor with opprest;
And, close as sin and suffering joined,
We march to fate abreast."

"Nearly sixteen millions of hands will aid you in pulling the load upward or they will pull against you the load downward. We shall constitute one-third and more of the ignorance and crime of the South or one-third its intelligence and progress. We shall contribute one-third to the business and industrial prosperity of the South or we shall prove a veritable body of death, stagnating, depressing, retarding, every effort to advance the body politic."

My own feeling is that the South will gradually reach the point where it will see the wisdom and the justice of enacting an educational or property qualification, or both, for voting, that shall be made to apply honestly to both races. The industrial development of the Negro in connection with education and Christian character will help to hasten this end. When this is done, we shall have a foundation, in my opinion, upon which to build a government that is honest and that will be in a high degree satisfactory to both races.

I do not suffer myself to take too optimistic a view of the conditions in the South. The problem is a large and serious one, and will require the patient help, sympathy, and advice of our most patriotic citizens, North and South, for years to come. But I believe that, if the principles which I have tried to indicate are followed, a solution of the question will come. So long as the Negro is permitted to get education, acquire property, and secure employment, and is treated with respect in the business or commercial world,— as is now true in the greater part of the South,— I shall have the greatest faith in his working out his own destiny in our Southern States. The education and preparing for citizenship of nearly eight millions of people is a tremendous task, and every lover of humanity should count it a privilege to help in the solution of a great problem for which our whole country is responsible.

AFRO-AMERICAN STUDIES
NEW AMERICAN LIBRARY · NEGRO UNIVERSITY PRESS

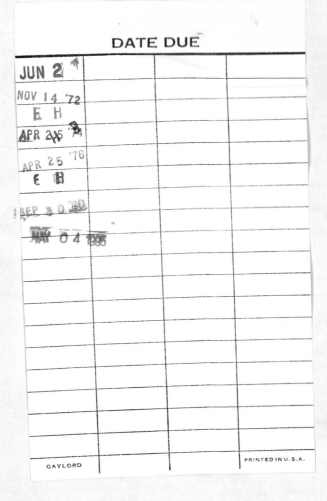

DATE DUE

JUN 2			
NOV 14 '72			
E H			
APR 25 '74			
APR 25 '76			
E H			
SEP 3 0 '90			
MAY 0 4 1995			
GAYLORD			PRINTED IN U.S.A.